Sioux City
REFLECTIONS OF SIOUXLAND PRIDE

Published by

SIOUX CITY
Journal

Ronald C. Peterson, Publisher

ISBN 0-9705534-0-4

Spanning the Missouri

Toll taker Fred Martin poses at the Combination Bridge in 1910 with his children, Ella, 5, Rose, 7, Lucy, 9, and Frank, 11. The view is from the Sioux City side looking south. The Combination Bridge was built in the 1890s and considered to be a marvel of its age. During opening ceremonies on the morning of Jan. 21, 1896, the south wing span of the bridge was scheduled to move apart in a dramatic demonstration of the new bridge's capabilities. It stuck on the very first attempt. The bridge served the community well until it was torn down and a new bridge, Siouxland Veterans Memorial Bridge, was opened on July 22, 1981. *(Submitted by Ginger Davenport, granddaughter of Fred Martin)*

The Sioux City Journal has reported and photographed the important and historic events of the Siouxland area since 1864.

This is not a local history book that focuses on the major news events and people starting with the "beginning" of Sioux City and then concluding with Sioux City "today." SIOUX CITY, REFLECTIONS OF SIOUXLAND PRIDE is our history as recorded in photos by the people themselves.

Selecting from the hundreds of photographs our neighbors generously loaned for this volume, we have tried to focus on everyday life in Sioux City. This book represents the men and women who built our community from the small river town of the past to the community we call home.

We hope you enjoy the view of life as it was in the eyes of those who made us what we are today.

Ronald C. Peterson
Publisher
Sioux City Journal

ACKNOWLEDGMENTS

Sioux City, Reflections of Siouxland Pride

Project Staff
Jessica Suing, Project Director
Larry Myhre, Book Editor
Jim Anderson, Project Assistant
Ranae Reed, Writer
Karen Luken, Copy Editor
Bruce Miller, Copy Editor
Stacey Schuetts, Photo Scanner
Angie Bohle, Graphic Artist

The Sioux City Public Museum
Daniel Truckey
Craig Olson
Grace Linden

And, most importantly,
to the hundreds of people who shared their photographs and memories.

Sioux City, Reflections of Siouxland Pride was a labor of love and to all those who helped in any way, we express our sincere appreciation. Special effort was made to ensure the accuracy of the information for each photograph. However, information written on the backs of photographs and dates recalled by contributors may not have been exact. For historical accuracy, we welcome corrected and additional information, which we will forward to the appropriate archives and museums. Please send changes to the Sioux City Journal, Book Department, Box 118, Sioux City, Iowa 51102.

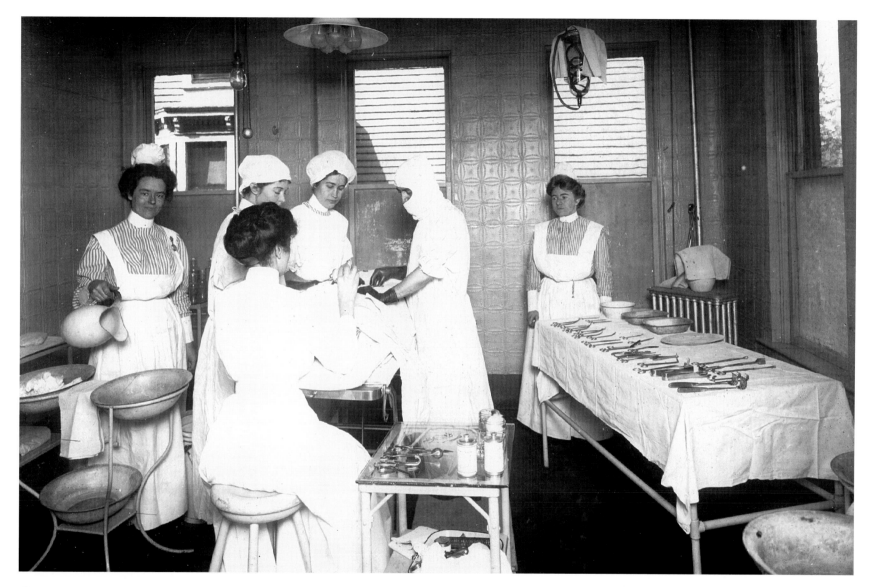

Breathe deeply

Surgical procedures have come a long way since this 1910 photo at Lutheran Hospital. Note the nurse in the foreground holding a container of ether. *(Submitted by St. Luke's Regional Medical Center)*

A 'Class' act

The 1939 fourth-grade class gathered outside Irving School for this group photo. The school remains in operation at 11th and Jennings streets. Front row from left, Jimmie, Arlie Sugget, Kenneth Burns, Richard, James Davis, Wallace, Roger Burke. Middle row, Delores, Ruth Wetzbarger, Margaret Olson, Shirley Tuton, Louise Parson, Henrietta Bennett, Bernadine, Delores Shearer. Third row, Jack Olson, Delores Chambers, Valerie T., Jimmie W., Vera, Edward Swanson, Gordon Roberts, George, Jackie S., Arlene (standing in back) Edward G., Charles Church, and Edmund. List of names was submitted by Shirley Tuton Swenson. *(Submitted by Dolores Shearer Sachau)*

Got Gas?

Mobil Gas, located at the northwest corner of Highway 75 and Leeds Avenue, was a full-service filling station owned and operated by Walter Pence. This 1942 photo shows Pence, right, and Doc Anderson, an employee, taking a brief break during their grand opening. *(Submitted by Maribel Smith, daughter of Walter Pence)*

Sunny days

The Sachau family enjoys an outing at Memorial Park Cemetery after church in 1952. From left, Delores Shearer Sachau, Harry Sachau, Julie Sachau Stickrod, Bobbette Sachau Theroux. *(Submitted by Delores Sachau)*

Sioux City 'Fonz'

Richard Anderson, a young bike enthusiast at the age of 19, strikes a pose on his 1938 Harley Davidson. Richard purchased his Harley from Albrecht Cycle Shop in the spring of 1940 for $300. Albrecht Cycle Shop was then located at 210 Fifth St. and is currently at 200 Fifth St. *(Submitted by Jim Anderson, son of Richard Anderson)*

Pioneering medical care

Samaritan Hospital was located on Pierce Street at the northwest corner of 17th Street as shown on this 1910 postcard. Established by the Women's Christian Association in 1875, it was the first true hospital in Northwest Iowa. It remained at its Pierce Street location until 1913 when the hospital was renamed "The New Samaritan" and relocated to 28th Street. *(Submitted by Dorothy Vander Weil)*

Boys of summer

Herbert Spencer, 5th from the right, joins several baseball teammates for a 1927 photograph for the Ryal Miller Chevrolet baseball club. Better known as Hibby, Herbert Spencer was a semi-pro player who was an inspiration to all young people who came in contact with the sport. Years later Herbert was inducted into the Sooland Softball Hall of Fame *(Submitted by Marge Camp daughter of Herbert Spencer)*

Ready for racin'

This is Riverview Park Speedway in 1946. It was located in the current Riverside Park area. The race track was used for midget car racing. It was a big attraction which always played to large audiences. Part of Riverside Amusement Park can be seen at right. *(Submitted by Russ Ross)*

Doggy timeout

In this 1918 photo of the late Louise Flynn Zerschling, about 3 years old, and her brother, Walter Flynn, 11, relax with their dog, Toby, in the front yard of their house on 18th St. Zerschling was a long-time Journal newsroom employee. *(Submitted by Lynn Zerschling, daughter of Louise Flynn Zerschling)*

The smokin' 1800s

This late 1800s photo shows the J.D. Engstrand Cigar Store located at 413 Jackson St. The owner was David J. Engstrand and the cigar maker was Swan Carlstrom. (*Submitted by Margaret Engstrand, granddaugher of David J. Engstrand*)

Peas in a pod

This photo taken in the late 1920s shows Emil Jahn, second from right, posing with some of his friends. They appear as if they are posing for a theatrical picture. (*Submitted by Dona Hicks*)

Devastation by water

The 1953 Floyd River flood destroyed many homes and businesses. The Sioux Soya Mill located on 11th Street at the southwest corner of Clark was one of those businesses.
(Submitted by Mary Thompson)

To the rescue

Many Sioux Cityans still remember the devastation of the 1953 Floyd River flood. Military trucks rescued many citizens by hauling them to safer ground. The flood hit so fast, many people had to be rescued from their rooftops.
(Submitted by Mary Thompson)

Cleaning up

This was the scene at Wilkins Pharmacy at 4001 Floyd Blvd. It was late that June 7, 1953 morning when the Floyd River hit the city with a surprising wall of water. Grover Wilkins, owner, stands at left. *(Submitted by Lola Brown)*

No boom bomb

Chuck Falkner, better-known as "Peewee," poses on a practice bomb for B-17 bombers in 1944 at the Sioux City Air Base. The bombers used the Missouri River as a reference point. Chalk was placed in the bombs so it could be determined if the target was hit. *(Submitted by Marvis Hendrickson)*

Early view of Morningside

Morningside College sits all alone in this 1902 photo. Charles Frances Eberly attended Morningside College from 1898 to 1902. He continued his education at other colleges. He received his teaching degree and worked as a pharmacist. *(Submitted by Debra Eberly, granddaughter-in-law of Charles Eberly)*

More starch, Mom

Catherine Furlich practices her ironing in 1953 at 2700 S. Cedar St., and looks as if she is pointed in the right direction.
(Submitted by Michael Furlich, father of Catherine Furlich)

Fun at the court

Tennis was a popular after hours and weekend pastime for these young ladies photographed around 1938. They are all members of the Sioux City Tennis Club which played at the Riverside Tennis Court. *(Submitted by Dwight Hauff)*

Li'l angel

Looking much like a little angel, Shirley Ann Carey stands on a rock outcropping in Stone Park in 1950. She was attending a family picnic near Dakota Point. *(Submitted by S.A. Watson, cousin of Shirley Ann Carey)*

Delivering the milk

This is the Soderstrom Dairy headquarters and one of the delivery trucks in a photo taken in the 1920s. Soderstrom Dairy was started in 1911 by Victor E. Soderstrom and in 1925 was turned over to Earl Soderstrom, in the truck. The dairy was located at 2701 Floyd Blvd., and the building now houses the Town House Lounge. *(Submitted by Lou Ann Soderstrom Eckert)*

A pair of Humphreys

In 1966 Vice President Hubert Humphrey, left, visited the Sioux City Stockyards and when told another Humphrey was in the room he wanted to meet him. That was Bob Humphrey, livestock salesman. Also pictured behind the Humphreys is Larry Wilds, left, and Bob Jensen. *(Submitted by Bob Humphrey)*

Girl on a bridge

Vivian Spencer strikes a pose on a foot bridge which connected Center and Silver streets. The photo was taken in the late 1920s. *(Submitted by Marge Camp)*

Hamburger, anyone?

Harry's Hamburger, also known as Harry's Cafe, was owned and operated by Harry S. Zanfes for 35 years at 719 Fourth St. The business was open 24 hours a day, seven days a week and didn't close for holidays. This photograph was taken in the late 1940s. *(Submitted by Marti Bostinelos)*

Tough little ladies

This is the 1937 Hawthorne School soccer team. Back row from left are Kathryn Speckman, Shirley Day, unidentified, Ida Coyle, Miss Enders (sixth grade teacher), Dorthy Mead, unidentified, and Norma Morrical. Front row from left are June Anderson Hebert, Ruth Carlberg, Zelta Miller, Phyllis Hittle, Florence Dommisse, Bernida Kinard and Dorothy Taylor. The photo was taken in front of Hawthorne School. *(Submitted by June Hebert)*

Backyard water fun

Cooling off on a hot day in 1963 are from left, Linda Wetzel, Lou Wetzel, Wynn Marshall and Douglas Furlich. The photo was taken in the 2600 block of South Cedar Street. *(Submitted by Michael Furlich, father of Douglas Furlich)*

1892 flood

In May of 1892, the Missouri River boiled out of its banks and laid waste to portions of Sioux City. This photo shows the railroad yards looking south from L Road. *(Submitted by Susan Francisco)*

Smithy at work

This blacksmith's shop was operated by Peter P. Simeon at 710 Sioux St., for several years. Simeon, left, did plow work, wagon work, general repairs and shoed horses. This photo was taken in 1894. *(Submitted by Marlene Kruse, daughter of Peter P. Simeon)*

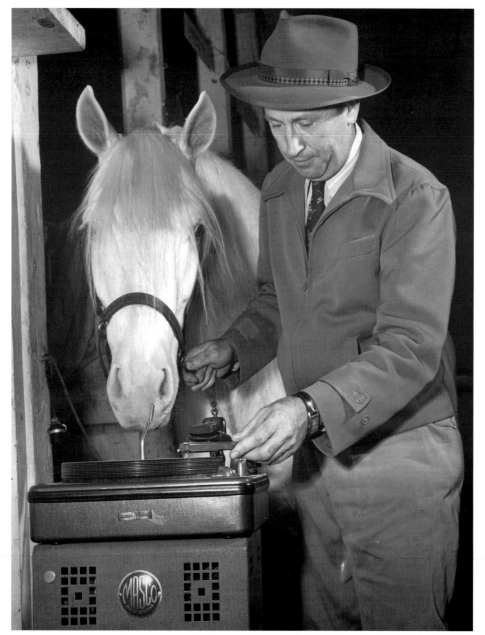

Early white horse

One of the earliest of the white horses of the famous White Horse Mounted Patrol is ridden above by Bernadine Bovee Wallin, left, and Mary Jo Peters Petronis in 1937. The photo was taken on Garretson Avenue across from Morningside College's Eppley Auditorium. *(Submitted by Mary Jo Petronis)*

Learning new tricks

Bob Taylor, trick horse trainer for Sioux City's famous White Horse Mounted Patrol, works with Silver Flash at the White Horse Mounted Patrol barn in the stockyards district. The photo was taken in the late 1940s or early 1950s. Silver Flash could count with his hooves and do other special tricks. Taylor is in Iowa's Horseman's Hall of Fame. *(Submitted by Janelle Carlson)*

Ready for grid action

This is the East High School football team of 1928. Front row from left are the unidentified assistant coach, unidentified, Virgil Moore, Keith Hatter, unidentified, Bill Huff, unidentified, unidentified, Bill Mahnke, and Les Davis, coach. Second row from left are Ernest Newman, Frank Johnson, unidentified, unidentified, Dwight Strom, George Bell, Robert Brown, unidentified and unidentified. Third row from left are Robert Howe, unidentified, Sam Epstein, unidentified, Leo Knutson, Ardin Hubbs, unidentified, unidentified and Ward Browning. *(Submitted by Donna Goehring)*

Master of the court

Herbert "Hibby" Spencer was one of the star players on the 1924 Central High School basketball team which won the state tournament that year. *(Submitted by Marge Camp)*

17

Softball, anyone?

This softball team was photographed outside the Tolerton and Warfield Building at Nebraska and Third streets in 1929. Front row from left are, (first name unknown) Foster, Bud Lymer, Virgil Moore, (first name unknown) Manzer, Al Pettit and Orville Farris. Back row from left are, Emmit Lobdell, Harold Storm, Frank Pettit, Bill Lymer, Willis Link, Cookie Manier and Benny Crain. *(Submitted by Donna Goehring)*

Water free, gas extra

Bob Wittern, left, and Levi Chedester were owners of the Riverside Conoco Service Station, 1756 Riverside Blvd., when the 1952 flood hit. They sold gas, hay, feed, rabbit food, coal and did mechanic work. There was a high demand for hay because many people in the area still had horses and the coal was sold to home owners for heating. Soda pop was 10 cents a bottle. *(Submitted by Fonda and Bob Chedester daughter-in-law and son-in-law of Levi Chedester)*

Ready to race

After World War II midget car races were at their peak. In 1955, Russ Ross drove No. 19 which sported a Ford V-8 engine. Enthusiasts could race in Sioux City, Cherokee, Council Bluffs, Fort Dodge and Des Moines, Iowa, and Luverne, Minn. *(Submitted by Russ Ross)*

The meat market

The CPI Meat Market was located at 617 Fourth St., in the late 1870s or early 1880s when this photograph was taken. Owner Charles Peter Ibs, standing in the doorway, was in the business at least 20 years. He slaughtered mostly cows and hogs and butchered them himself.
(Submitted by Robert Ibs, son of Charles Peter Ibs)

Heavy hitter likes golf

Left, Ken Donohue, and right, Joe Louis, heavyweight boxer, take time for this 1948 photo. Louis was in town visiting the Donohue family and took time out for a round of golf. *(Submitted by Ken Donohue)*

Tragedy at Swift

A vicious explosion ripped into the Swift and Co., plant on Dec. 14, 1949. Twenty employees and a truck driver were killed and 91 were injured. Al Molskow, member of the Sioux City Fire Department, was not on duty that day but was only one block away when the blast occurred and snapped this photograph. *(Submitted by Al Molskow)*

Westside view

This photograph offers a view of Sioux City from the westside in this early 1900s photo. *(Submitted by Vivian Stone Fox)*

Fun at the Shamrock Inn

Marie "Peewee" Westendorf was a waitress at the Shamrock Inn, 801 W. Seventh St., in 1937 where she served sandwiches. The establishment was owned by Louie Klameth. The building is now occupied by Lessman's Lighting Center. *(Submitted by Helen Miller, daughter of Marie Westendorf)*

A Christmas party

Students at Lowell School gather for a group photograph before their Christmas party in 1929. The program included singing of Christmas carols, reciting, playing, gift exchanging and other entertainment in keeping with the season. *(Submitted by Dave Gordon)*

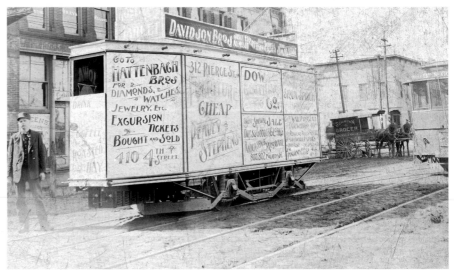

A rolling billboard

This advertising streetcar rented out for $400 a month. Photo was taken between 1895 and 1900. A portable organ inside the car played music to draw the attention of passersby. (*Submitted by Dave Bishop)*

Beauticians all

Students at Samuel's School of Beauty Culture gather for a group portrait in 1941. Manager of the school was Noah Lewin, center, and the school's single instructor was Blanche Tone, second row, sixth from left. The school was represented as being the oldest and best school in the Northwest, serving the states of Minnesota, South Dakota, Nebraska and Iowa. It was located at 509 Fourth St. (*Submitted by Elaine Shanahan*)

A sales lineup

Ten salesmen for the Sioux City Seed and Nursery Company line up for a group photo in 1917. The firm was located at the northeast corner of 20th and Clark streets. (*Submitted by Dave Gordon*)

Early automobile repairs

This is the Smith Brothers Automobile Repair shop at 504 Court St. about 1920. The shop was owned by Harry W. and James E. Smith. The shop relocated to this site in a building they constructed for their business. In the photo third from left are: Heinie Swanson and Jim Smith. Others are unidentified. *(Submitted by Mary Helen McElroy, daughter of Heinie Swanson)*

A first at stockyards

The first black Angus cattle to be delivered to the Sioux City stockyards was shipped by Chris Smith, Jackson, Neb., (shown behind the cattle facing the camera). The black Angus breed was docile and considered at the time to be the best for human consumption. *(Submitted by Alfred A. Smith, grandson of Chris Smith)*

Dancin' away fourth grade

Fourth graders in Hopkins School, 916 W. Eighth St., practice dancing in this 1950 photo. Dancers from left are Phyllis Habben, Dick Wilmot; Phyllis Yates, Jerry Ferguson; Sandra Mercer, John Hillman; Clyde Leedom, Diane O'Sullivan; Idabell Olson, Claude Leedom; and Henry Fields, Ella Mary Goetsch. Seated from left are Lawrence LeClair, Lewis Wilmot, Dick Mathison, Jules Smith and Darwin Johnson. *(Submitted by Donna Fritch Fuller)*

You name it, we got it

Lyman Eugene "L.E." Carnes Co. was located at 407 W. Seventh St., now Kollman Appliance. L.E. owned and managed the dry goods store pictured in the early 1900s. *(Submitted by Marilyn Johnson, granddaughter of L.E. Carnes).*

Girls not allowed

Johnny Tracy, left, Bob Lowndes, Grayson Sweeley and Ed Lowndes pose in front of their clubhouse in this 1930 photo. All four boys took part in building the clubhouse. Remember, "No Girls Allowed." *(Submitted by Pat Lowndes, wife of Bob)*

Keeping up with the times

L.E. Carnes Co., a dry goods store, was located at 407 W. Seventh St., where this photograph was taken in 1903 or 1904. The building was later renovated and turned into the Palace Theatre. Mr. Carnes would charge 5 cents for a movie. *(Submitted by Marilyn Johnson)*

Let the party begin

Employees of S.S. Kresge's Co., get ready to celebrate Christmas in 1924 on the first floor of the store, where you could shop and enjoy a soda when you were done. *(Submitted by Ruth Blake)*

Wild blue yonder

Tri-State Airlines Inc. would give people a 15 minute plane ride for $3. Tri-State became Hamford Airlines. The plane on the left was known as Miss Sioux City. *(Late 1920s photo submitted by Jack Fleckenstein)*

Three good friends

Millie Raveling, left, Shirley Tuton and Louise Parsons posed for their 1947 graduation photo. *(Submitted by Shirley Tuton Swenson)*

Early log cabin

Theophile Bruguier's Cabin was moved to this location at 1075 Council Oak Drive in Feburary and March of 1934. It was completed in the fall and spring of 1935 and 1936. The cabin was dedicated in June 1936 for use by the Girls of '68 Junior Pioneers as a clubhouse. Pictured in the doorway of this 1935 photo are, Julia Sokoloff, president, and Emma Knittel, vice president. Theophile Bruguier was the first white settler in Sioux City. *(Submitted by Marvis Hendrickson)*

The Smith house

The Smith House is located at 1705 Rebecca St. The house is next door to Smith School. The lady on the porch is Rebecca Smith, for which Rebecca Street was named. The men are workers who completed the house about 1875. The first owners were the Smiths. The second owner was Harold Edwards. Edwards purchased the home from the Smith's estate for $8,000 in 1960. The photo was taken in the late 1800s. *(Submitted Vickie Henrichsen, daughter of Harold Edwards)*

Let's all come together

This 1944-1945 photo was taken at the Masonic Temple. The All School Music Festival invited all schools from Sioux City to make music. Henri Pensis, director and conductor, was the conductor of the Sioux City Symphony from 1942 to 1946. He also taught instrumental music at Morningside College. *(Submitted by George Burg)*

Augustana Lutheran Church

Swedish Lutheran Augustana Church was built in 1876 at Fifth and Virginia streets. The pipe organ was built by Lars Molene, a member of the congregation. This photo was taken in 1882. The church had about 170 people in the congregation. *(Submitted by Augustana Lutheran Church)*

Palmer candy

Harry W. Smith, second from the left, and eight co-workers at the Palmer Candy Co., pose for this photo. Palmer candy opened in 1878. They made boxed chocolates, hand-dipped chocolates, hand dipped cherries, lemon drops, etc. This photo was taken at 209 Douglas St., which was a four story building built in 1899. In 1904, a fifth floor was added and the Palmer family legend has it that one of the family members lived on the fifth floor and would occasionally bring his horse and buggy up with him. The Palmer Candy Co., is now located at 311 Bluff St. Palmer Candy is a five generation business of family ownership. *(Submitted by Harry Smith's niece, Mary Helen McElroy)*

Lucky Lindy

Charles Lindbergh, left, meets Mayor Gilman. The city gave a big parade and banquet at the Martin Hotel in Sioux City in Lindbergh's honor. Lindbergh was in Sioux City a day and a half following his Atlantic Ocean flight. They are pictured here at the North Sioux City Airport in 1927. *(Submitted by Jack Fleckenstein)*

Davidson Bros. Co.

This popular department store, Davidson Bros. Co., was located at Fourth and Pierce streets. This 1932 photo taken on the second floor shows the ready-to-wear gowns that were available to shoppers. If you needed a fancy dress, this was the place to shop. During the Christmas season, Davidson's would have a beautiful window display for the shoppers to view. *(Submitted by Pat Mustain)*

Classmates and buddies

In 1946 Marge Fitzpatrick, left, Patricia Tierney, Mary Nelson, Patty Mann, Mary Jane Sheehan and Marian Schmidt pose on the steps of St. Joseph's Nursing Home. They were attending St. Joseph Mercy College of Nursing at the time. *(Submitted by Mary Jane Anderson)*

Right this way

Ushers from the Orpheum Theater are shown in this 1939 photo. From left are Kay Beechem, Pat Marksbury, Jimmy Curry, Ralph Thorp, Frank Mullin, Bob Stark, John Lynch, Ed Lilly, Wayne Murray, Orville Lee, Richard Jones, John Zink and Jimmy Alexander. The ushers were paid 25 cents an hour. They were paired up to change the marquee which notified people of upcoming shows. *(Submitted by Marie Stark, wife of Bob Stark)*

Just a step away

This 1902 photo, taken in Cole's Addition on the east side of Sioux City, is of the Alex Johnson family who resided at what was then 820 Plymouth St. The name of the street was later changed to Lewis Boulevard. Their home was located next door to a small grocery store which they operated for more than 20 years. It was then converted into a home. Pictured are Martha, Anna, Elsie, Alex, Mary holding Helen, Howard and Archie. *(Submitted by Robert Hansen, son of Martha Johnson)*

Line up, inspection time

It was time to line up for inspection in 1949 when the children of George and Bernice Gengler, 1328 S. Alice St., were getting ready for their first day of school. The children from left are Jeanne, Robert, Carole, Ken, Jim, Leo, Helen and Mary Jo. They attended Immaculate Conception Grade School at 3719 Ridge Ave. *(Submitted by Robert Gengler's wife, Mary Lou Gengler)*

The boat stops here

Former President Harry Truman walks in front of the Sergeant Floyd riverboat during a visit to Sioux City in 1960. *(Submitted by Sioux City Public Museum)*

Ready to eat

Members of the Pioneer Club attended a dinner at Davidson's Tea Room on April 23, 1924. At the speaker's table on the extreme right are, Dr. Charles E. Snyder, Monsignor Thomas McCarty, Mrs. Mercy Bonnin, Conger Bonnin and Sam Bruguier, son of Theophile Bruguier. *(Submitted by Sioux City Public Museum)*

Pedaling away

These are members of the Inter-Ocean Wheel or Cycling Club in 1900. Standing, from left are, Andy Lagger, Will Duncan, Alf Hills, Tom Rae, W.J. Ashley, Charlie Ellis, Johnnie Lessenich, Charles Miller, Charles Hughson, unknown, Charlie Ashley. Sitting from left, Frank Monfort, William Bowser, unknown, Art Hughson, George Brooks and Stanley Johnson. Small boy at left front is George Meierstein. Small boy at right front, is F.B. Ashley. Lying on the ground, Clyde Davis. *(Submitted by Sioux City Public Museum)*

He's sooo cute!

This is the Grand Auction of the Little Yellow Dog mascot on Wednesday, Dec. 23, 1942, at the Martin Hotel. From left are Don Cunningham, auctioneer, Joellen Twohig and the successful bidder, Hugh J. Twohig of Wagner, Garrison and Abbott commission firm. *(Submitted by Sioux City Public Museum)*

Spanning time

The Combination Bridge was completed in 1896 and is shown in this photo. In the background is the ferryboat/tender "Capitol" and the Pontoon Bridge is being dismantled. The Combination Bridge was torn down during the years from 1978-1981. Covington, Neb., is shown in the background. This 1896 photo was taken from Prospect Hill. *(Submitted by Sioux City Public Museum)*

A caring attitude

This is the class of 1949 from St. Joseph Mercy School of Nursing at 2217 Court St. Students would attend the three-year course to receive their registered nurse's degree. For the first year, students from Sioux City, Fort Dodge and Mason City, Iowa, all attended classes together. In their second and third year, they would attend classes in their own towns. *(Submitted by Jane Dalton)*

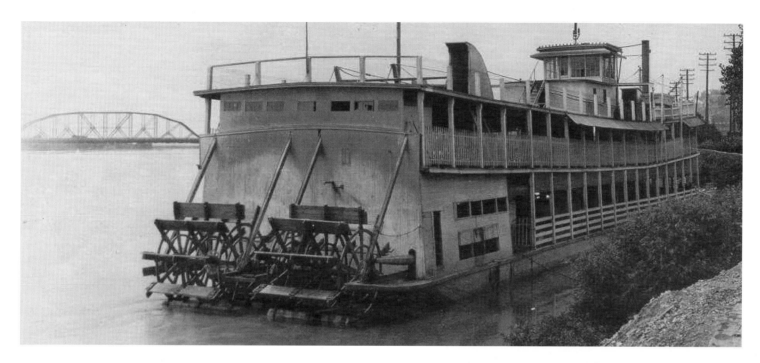

Old man river

Boat "John Heckmann" was a sternwheel, wooden-hull steamboat built at Hermann, Mo., in 1919. She had two sternwheels operated by four Gillette and Eaton engines. A big carrier for her size, she was owned by the Heckmann family with Captain Ed Heckmann master. The boat was rebuilt into an excursion boat for the Missouri River and was lost in the ice at Hermann in 1928. *(1927 photo submitted by Sioux City Public Museum)*

The more, the merrier

In 1907 this was the largest family in Sioux City with 15 children. Henry and Julia Pegar Fachman were the proud parents of Julius, Virginia, Eliza, Edward, Robert, William, Hennrietta, Ruth, Fred, George, Eva, Dolly, Mark, Charles and Frank. The couple met in 1866. He fell in love with her at first sight, proposed to her on the spot and they were married that afternoon. Photo is from the late 1800s. *(Submitted by Kathleen Saxe)*

And the band plays on

The 1938 Monahan Post Band poses in front of City Hall. (*Submitted By George Burg*)

Cheering the way

Cathy Wilen, Cathy Johnson, Sandy Adams and Kathy Osterholt ride in the Central High School Homecoming parade in this 1969 photo. The girls were Central High School's football cheerleaders. (*Submitted by Cathy Wilen Podwysocki*)

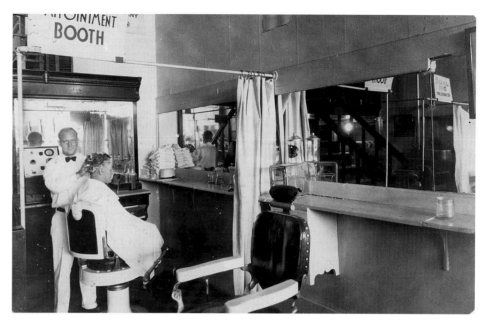

Chow time

Tony Primates and his granddaughter, Elaine Diavates, pose for this 1952 photo in front of Frisco Lunch. The owner was Tony Stamoulis. His son-in-law, Tony Primates, worked with him for the couple of years the cafe was open. *(Submitted by Georgia Diavates, mother of Elaine.)*

Just a little off the sides

Sioux City Barber College was located at 925 Fourth St., where this photo was taken in 1931. Herbert H. Smith, known as "Red," was the manager of the college for 40 years. Following World War II, he attended barber school in New York and found his way to Sioux City. The college was open six days a week from 7 a.m. to 11 p.m. The college was destroyed in a fire in 1972. *(Submitted by Katie Batcheller, daughter of Herbert H. Smith.)*

A day in the park

From left, Bev Hayes, Delores Peters, Millie Bollig, Butch Wessling, Beverly and Dorothy Fitzpatrick were photographed in 1949 in front of the Riverside Amusement Park. The park contained a fun house, roller coaster, concession stands, bumper cars and a Ferris wheel. *(Submitted by Millie Kisting)*

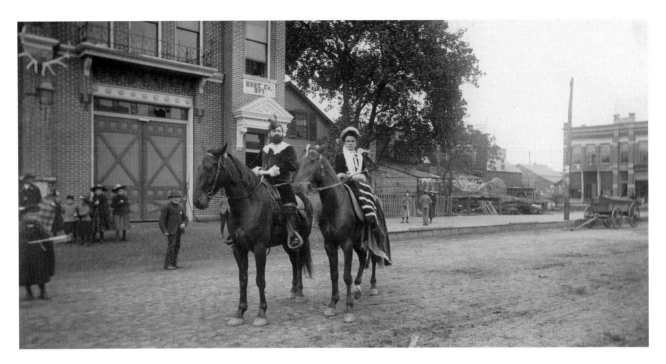

Queen of the Parade

Mrs. John Holdenreid was named Queen of the Parade in this late 1800s photo taken in front of Fire Hose House 1. The king is unknown. *(Submitted by Frances Sulzbach)*

Need a lift?

Frank B. Murphy is shown in this 1930 photo in front of his cab at 411 11th St. Frank worked for Checker Taxi Co., located at 224 Fourth St., for about 20 years. *(Submitted by his daughter, Verna Wilen)*

Pass the cookies

In 1956, Ken Wayman, anchorman at Channel 4, was asked by Girl Scout Troop 23 to be their guest at a luncheon at the Girl Scouts' Camp. *(Submitted by Georgia Diavates)*

All aboard

Employees of Chicago Northwestern Railroad pose for this 1935 photo. The photo was taken at 124 Nebraska St. Shown here are the freight office staff. *(Submitted by Verna Wilen)*

Double the fun

Grace Wright and Blanche Sewellon pose for this 1914 photo taken in Grandview Park. The girls were on a double date and decided to view the flowers. *(Submitted by Geri Day, daughter of Grace Wright)*

Literary hound

Larry Fuller and Peggy, his Boston bulldog, take time to share a book in this 1940 photo. Larry thought Peggy would be able to read better if she had her glasses on. *(Submitted by Larry Fuller)*

41

Clang, clang, clang goes the trolley

This is the first group of trainmen (streetcar conductors) to receive five-year Safety Award Buttons on Sept. 20, 1943, in Sioux City. The awards were presented in a ceremony at the Warrior Hotel by G.A. Neal. From left, first row: Otto Rice, William Pryor, John St. Rong, Walter Haefs, Walter Noyes, Joseph Ploof and Mike Kaiser. Second row: Earl Garnett, Oliver Barboe, Chris Bern, L.L. Cormany, E.E. Rhoads, Harry Dam, John Ploof. Third row: Ray Ruhleman, George Spencer, George Thorngreen, Percy Beorman, William Tripp, G.O. Oliver, N.L. Teske, Herman Muir. Not pictured were Clyde Terrill and J.H. Griffen. *(Submitted by Phyllis Schwagerl, daughter of streetcar conductor George Thorngreen)*

Just a little dip

Audrey and JoAnn Brown decided the best way to cool down on a hot summer day was to take a little dip in the washtub in this mid-1930s photo. Wally Lenz must have had the same idea but was a little late. *(Submitted by Pat Duff, cousin of Audrey and Jo Ann)*

Now that's a hog

Charyl Alvey O'Brien, 3, sits on her dad's Harley Davidson motorcycle at her home at 2417 Lakeport St., in this 1948 photograph. She would often ride with her father. *(Submitted by Evelyn Alvey, mother of Charyl Alvey O'Brien)*

Family affair

Steve, Kerry, Connie, George and Kristy Wilen are getting ready to go on a family bike ride in this 1964 photo. The picture was taken at 3011 Valley Drive. Steve and George are now co-owners of Jetsun Aviation and both have their pilot's license. *(Submitted by George's mother, Verna Wilen)*

Blast from the past

Harry Spidell shows off his centennial outfit for the Sioux City Centennial parade in 1954. He posed outside of Weatherwax, 600 Fourth St., where he was employed. Weatherwax offered men's clothing and furnishings. *(Submitted by Sandra Lynch, niece of Harry Spidell)*

Inside the works

Charles Burns, W.H. Burns and an unidentified worker pose for this late 1800s photo. They were employed with S.C. Cornice Works at 412 Water St. The business was established in 1884. The company worked with copper, slate and tin. *(Submitted by Katie Colling, great-granddaughter of William H. Burns)*

Big dreams

This is the 1943 kindergarten class at St. Boniface Catholic School, 712 W. Sixth St., First row from left: Mahala Garrigan, Connie O'Dea, Deanna Dais, Ann Scully, Jackie Leinhart, Marjean Treft and Janice Baker. Second row: Gerald Hansel, unknown, Peggy Echols, Theresa McKenzie, unknown, Patricia Levering, unknown and unknown. Third row: Bill McInerney, Michael Delancy, unknown, Ronald Chicoine, unknown, unknown and unknown. Fourth row: unknown, Gelad Tritz, unknown, unknown and Leo Peterson. Fifth row: unknown, unknown, Bill Bogaard, unknown and Kenny Baker. (Submitted by Jackie Leinart Davis)

A hand up

During 1933 and 1934, times were hard so the W.P.A. Project was developed to provide jobs. These workers are tearing down the hill on Rustin Street and Leech Avenue to build homes. (Submitted by Dorothea Korstad Kroll)

Doggone hot

Jody and Judy Sperling and Lori and Cindy Duff decide the best way to cool off on a hot day was to give the dog a bath. By the time they finished this 1964 idea, the kids were wetter than the dog. (Submitted by Pat Duff, mother of Lori and Cindy)

Strollin' along

Vern Pranke takes a stroll downtown on Fourth Street near the Kresge dime store in 1950. *(Submitted by Julie Miller-Pranke)*

The Sultan of Swat and friends

Baseball legends Babe Ruth and Lou Gehrig were in Sioux City in 1927 visiting John Donohue, 3723 Jackson St., when this photo was taken in Donohue's backyard. From left are James Donohue, Babe Ruth, Phil Donohue, Lou Gehrig holding Ken Donohue. *(Submitted by Ken Donohue, son of John Donohue)*

Ready, set, hut, hut

Members of the East High School 1931 football team posed in their new uniforms at the stockyards football field. First row from left, Coach Davis, Marple, Hakenholz, Pederson, J. Anderson, Muth, Rasmussen, McKenzie, Needham, R. Anderson and Coach Stevens. Second row: Hollmer, Crippen, Doidge, Stromlund, Lindblade, McConnell, Hayse, Griffith, Pakeltis, Humphrey and Cooper. Third Row: Carroll, Burney Bilunos, Showaltler, Gregalunus, Arnold, Kriss, James, Thorpe and Peterson. East High's record for that year was 6-3-1. *(Submitted by Paul Bilunos)*

Stringing it along

Alex Goodrich, center, was employed with Cudahy Packing Co., as a sausage maker for more than 30 years. He is pictured here with his co-workers in 1935. *(Submitted by Alex's grandson, Paul Bilunos)*

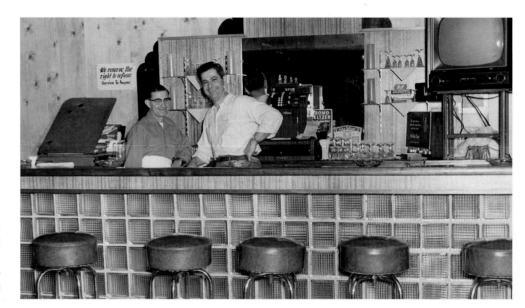

Sit back and relax

Danny's Place is shown in this 1951 photo. Located at 2910 Military Road, it was known for its aged steaks. Danny is shown on the right. *(Submitted by his daughter, Ellen Ayers)*

Keep the lights on

George Fisher, second from right, was employed as an electrician with Sioux City Gas and Electric Co., located at 507-511 Pierce St. The company supplied many Sioux City homes with natural gas. Early 1900s photo. *(Submitted by George's grandson, Duane Meier)*

From D.C. to S.C.

Eugene Kelly, left, Ed Haakinson, Eugene F. Kelly and John C. Kelly are pictured in this 1935 photo taken at the Sioux City Rail Depot near 100 Pierce St. The Kellys owned the Sioux City Tribune, which later merged with the Sioux City Journal in 1942. Haakinson, a former Tribune employee, was a Washington correspondent. He was in Sioux City to deliver a speech to the Chamber of Commerce. *(Submitted by Katie Kelly Colling)*

A proud moment

The graduating class of 1936 was photographed in front of Cathedral High School located at 1002 Grandview Blvd. Cathedral was an all-girls school until years later when Bishop Heelan High School was built. Heelan became a co-ed parochial school. Cathedral offered the girls tap dance, vocal music and instrumental lessons for an additional fee. *(Submitted by Elvira Alvarez)*

Flying high

Charles F. Hanson shown in this early 1900s photo, proudly displays his plane. Charles was the first Sioux Cityan to personally own his own plane. The plane was shipped from Cincinnati, Ohio, and Charles assembled it himself. The last known location of this plane was the Ford Museum in Detroit. *(Submitted by Charles' son, Earl Hanson)*

Tall ears

Carlotta, right, and John Doneldson show what a bumper crop of corn should look like in this 1874 photo. The couple migrated from Sweden in 1873 and lived outside of Leeds. *(Submitted by Lucille Spurlock)*

Hope arrives

In the early 1950s, when most people were leaving Sioux City because of the polio epidemic, Bob Hope, center, was arriving. The Junior Chamber of Commerce welcomed Bob. Pictured are, from left, back row, Frank Dugan, Elloitt Wooldridge, Elmer Swenson, unknown, Bob Hope, Bob Hutmacher, Del Stone and Jack Larson. The last two men and those in the front row are not identified. *(Submitted by Vivian Stone Fox)*

Let's eat

Danny's Place at 2910 Military Road, was owned by Danny Baker, center back. He poses with his staff in this 1952 photo. The restaurant served steak, prime rib and spaghetti. If you wanted to go out and meet good people and eat good food, Danny's was the place. *(Submitted by Danny's daughter, Ellen Ayers)*

Gone but not forgotten

Pilot Lt. Warren Brown, second from the right, receives his briefing while serving with the 185th Air National Guard in 1968. He left for Vietnam the next day. He was killed in action two months after arriving. *(Submitted by Pat Feldich)*

Beers away

Ray V. Mitchell, a local beer distributor, stands in front of one of his trucks in this 1949 photo taken at 300 Court St. His trucks were insured with Joe Morten and Son Insurance Agency. *(Submitted by Great West Casualty)*

Happy trails

This 1934 photo of George Wilen Jr., age 3, was taken at 110 Main St. Businessmen would go to local neighborhoods and give pony rides and take pictures of the children. *(Submitted by Verna Wilen)*

A place for the night

The Mountaineer House, shown in this late 1800s photo, was located at 914 Fourth St. It was operated by William E. Tabke and his family. If you needed a clean room and a hot meal, this was the hotel for you. *(Submitted by Adele Wood, great-granddaughter of William E. Tabke)*

Taking a break

Millie Bollig Kisting takes a break while cleaning up flood waters in the Livestock National Bank where she was a personal loan teller. The 1953 flood took the workers by surprise. The bank employees formed a hand line to get out of the building to higher ground. *(Submitted by Millie Kisting)*

Moo-ving on

Bennie Ivener, left, Red Deets and Tom Ivener pose in this 1937 photo in front of Ivener Bros. Packing Co. at 825 S. Lafayette St. Tom and Bennie were co-owners of the packing company. Bennie later sold the business to Meyer Epstein and the business then became Meyer Packing Co. *(Submitted by Michelle Ivener, daughter-in-law of Bennie Ivener)*

Ahchoo

In this 1954 photo, Catherine Furlich is all dressed up to attend the Sioux City Centennial, but a summer cold may ruin the day for her. *(Submitted by Catherine's father, Michael Furlich)*

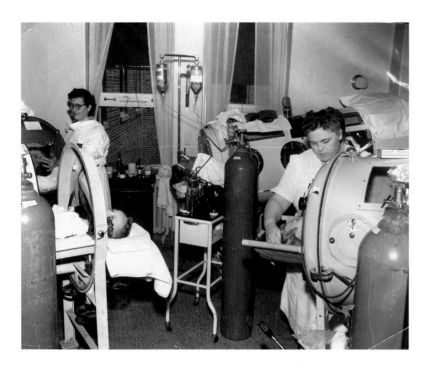

The iron lung

During the polio outbreak in the 1950s, many children had to use a machine known as the "Iron Lung" to help them breathe. Gordon Greta, 6, left, was one of those children in this 1952 photo taken at St. Joseph's Hospital, 2101 Court St. Gordon was kept in the "Iron Lung" for six weeks and missed an entire school year. He was home schooled. *(Submitted by Glendy Nichols)*

Presidential seat

Lori Fortner sits on the shoulders of Charles Ellison as she awaits the arrival of presidential candidate Barry Goldwater in 1964. On Charles' right is Yvonne Beck. At his left is J.E. "Ed" Goettsch. Lori Fortner Bowitzer is now an elementary art teacher in the Sioux City school system. *(Submitted by Yvonne Beck)*

Giddy-up goat

Mary Louise Kruger Musselman enjoyed a goat cart ride in 1933 or 1934 at her home at 4400 Tyler St. A man brought his goat to Leeds and gave the kids a ride. *(Submitted by Wendy Oldenkamp, daughter of Mary Louise)*

Birthday boy

Larry Fuller is enjoying his new birthday present from his Aunt Beth in 1939. Decked out in his hat and sweater, he looks ready to go to work in the garden. *(Submitted by Donna Fuller, wife of Larry Fuller)*

Early Rotary

This is a photo of a Rotary Club luncheon meeting which was hosted by Len O'Harrow at 902 Fourth St., sometime between 1914 and 1916. Arc lights lit the meeting room until 1916. The club was organized Oct. 1, 1912. Mr. O'Harrow is standing, seventh from left. *(Submitted by Adele Wood, granddaughter of Len O'Harrow)*

Scherling Drug

This early 1930s photograph shows the interior of Scherling Drug, 1201 Fourth St. The store sold drugs, paints, oils, glass and candies. Its soda fountain was also popular. *(Submitted by Gloria Hansen)*

Pick of the litter

Bruce A. Hardy, 6, 210 W. 24th St., proudly displays his three new puppies in this 1941 photo. *(Submitted by Delores Bogenrief)*

Smile

Jim Duff, 9, saddled up to have his picture taken in 1948 at his grandmother's residence at 14th and Virginia streets. A gentleman would go from neighborhood to neighborhood and give kids a pony ride. He would then provide a cowboy hat and take the child's picture. *(Submitted by Pat Duff)*

Day at the zoo

Lloyd Elkins Sr., and Clara Elkins are spending a day at the zoo at Stone State Park in 1930. They would visit the zoo occasionally to see the animals and enjoy some time together. *(Submitted by Darlene Elkins Olson)*

Something to sing about

The Abu-Bekr Chanters sing their way down the Sioux City parade route in this downtown 1970 photo. Don Kelsey is the director. Throughout the years, the Shriners have raised thousands of dollars for children with orthopedic problems, cleft disorders and burns. *(Submitted by Abu-Bekr Temple)*

Afternoon drive

Mike Davis and his mother, Jackie, pose in this 1958 photo taken in Stone State Park on Dakota Point. *(Submitted by Jackie Davis)*

What a deal

William Warnock Co., 216 Sixth St., shown in this 1918 photo, repaired and sold cars in the Warnock Building, which is now the Benson Building. Frank D. Reed, left, worked as a salesman with the company for 14 years. Frank and other salesmen would go out East and each man would drive a new car back to the showroom. *(Submitted by Margaret Bennett, daughter of Frank Reed)*

Life on the farm

Mark Ayers holds his little brother Bill as they scoot on their little red wagon in the late 1950s. Life on the farm was tough, but the boys were making the best of a difficult time. *(Submitted by Mark Ayers)*

The horse sees all

The White Horse Mounted Patrol was in a big parade when Imperial Sir Harold Lloyd came to Sioux City in 1948. Harold Lloyd wore glasses, so the Shriners thought it would be a neat idea to put glasses on the horses. The Abu-Bekr Temple was organized in March 1907 and has grown to a membership of more than 3,200 in much of western Iowa. *(Submitted by the Abu-Bekr Temple)*

Steady

A.R. Brostrom was a jeweler in Sioux City in the late 1930s. He was an independent jeweler and manufactured and repaired jewelry for more than 40 years. *(Submitted by Frances Marx, daughter of A.R. Brostrom)*

Fill 'er up

Aaron Foix was a gas station attendant at Red Devil Oil Co., in the early 1930s. Gas was just 12 cents a gallon. The Red Devil was a full service station located at W. Seventh and Market streets. *(Submitted by Ed Foix)*

Majestic home

This is the home of H.A. Jandt on the northeast corner of Sixth and Jennings streets. The home was built in 1881. Jandt and his wife had nine children who grew up in the home. Jandt ran a wholesale dry goods store located at Fourth and Pearl streets. *(Submitted by Betty Dobyns and Janet Hansen)*

Dress right, dress
Members of the Sioux City Police Department are lined up for an inspection in this 1962 photo. *(Submitted by Anthony Bilunas)*

Lazy Sunday afternoon
Mary Ann, Nancy and Carolyn Galusha, from left, take a break with their dog, Boxer, on a Sunday afternoon. Nancy and Carolyn were not twins but the two dressed alike. This 1951 photo was taken at their residence at 923 S. Mulberry St. *(Submitted by Nancy Peterson)*

Sioux City to Chitown

"Hiawatha" was a diesel train that went through Sioux City in the early 1940s. Better known as the last car of the Hiawatha, this was a passenger train that went from Sioux City to Chicago. *(Submitted by Norvin Rickman)*

Calling all crews

Gordon Moss, third from right, was employed with J.H. Keeffe Construction, the company that built the telephone building at Ninth and Douglas streets in 1926. *(Submitted by Jeannette Lubsen)*

On his way up

Maj. J.A. Konopisos, left, and Lt. Colonel Don Forney, right, promote Richard J. Marx from senior master sergeant to captain with the 185th Fighter Group in this mid 1960s photo. *(Submitted by Frances Marx, wife of Richard Marx)*

Where's the beef?

Barney Baron and Sons at 405 Fourth St., was an elite market in Sioux City as shown in this 1931 photo. When you walked into the market, you would walk on wood chips. They were a full-line grocery store. You could get a pound of bologna for 10 cents and a pound of minced ham for 15 cents. To wait on you were, from left, Bob Funley, Bill Karcher, who was the sausage maker, and Jim Harwood. *(Submitted by Leo Wagner)*

An ounce of prevention

John Pettit, supervisor in the curing department of Swift and Co., stands ready with sandbags filled in case the Missouri River would undercut and wash out sections of earth fill made in preparation for the 1952 flood. *(Submitted by Donald Molden, brother-in-law to John Pettit)*

Best friends

Jim Duff, 7, and his dog, Tip, are out for a walk in 1946. The photo was taken at Sixth and Virginia streets. *(Submitted by Kris Weigel)*

Take me to the river

The Perry Creek flood in July 1909, left hundreds of homes and businesses in ruins. Barney Conlin and Leo Bethscheider drowned in the churning waters. Doctors feared with the clean-up would come cases of typhoid and malaria. This photo was taken at Third Street, downtown and looking west. The Battery Building is to the left.
(Submitted by Jeannette Lubsen)

Ted's Cafe

Ted's Cafe, 5404 Military Road, was owned by Elmer C. Colt, better-known as "Ted." He is shown in the 1930s, at right. Standing behind the counter are Wayne Patton, waiter, and Nell Bonner, cook. Seated at the counter are Ray Chose, Laverne Suffield and Evelyn Colt. *(Submitted by Evelyn Colt Pleuger, daughter of Ted Colt)*

After the races

The Chesterfield Lounge, 418 Nebraska St., was a popular after-the-races spot in 1946 for those competing at Riverview Race Track. George Binnie, one of the top racecar drivers in the United States at the time, is shown parked in front of the lounge. The lounge was located next to the Capitol Theater. *(Submitted by Russell Ross)*

Making serum

Cliff Carlson, left, and two unidentified men were hog shacklers at Allied Laboratory, 1100 Bluff Road, in 1947. Their job was to collect blood from hogs for the manufacture of serum products sold by the firm. *(Submitted by Richard "Red" Betz)*

Soapbox racer

This is Walter T. Flynn in 1914 posing with his soapbox racer. Walter made the cars for his brothers and neighborhood friends while grow-ing up on the near northside. On July 4, 1914, Walter got to meet the famous race car driver Eddie Rickenbacker after he won a $10,000 purse at the speedway in North Sioux City. Upon seeing Walter's soapbox vehicle, Rickenbacker commented, "That is a mighty fine looking car you have there young man." Walter later became a dentist in Sioux City and Rickenbacker went on to become a celebrated World War I flying ace. *(Submitted by Stuart W. Flynn, son of Dr. Walter T. Flynn)*

Ice cream for sale.

This is the Roe Dairy Store in 1947, located on Pierce Street. The man at left is Judd Follett. Founded in 1941, Roe Dairy manufactured ice cream and even offered home delivery up to 1947. In 1947, hand-packed ice cream sold for 52 cents a quart and 30 cents a pint. The business was owned by Orrie and Bud Roe. The firm was in business until 1973. *(Submitted by Bob Roe, son of Orrie Roe)*

Ready to board

Mrs. McGovern, left, in car, Sgt. Edwinna McGovern, Dr. McGovern and Elaine Homan are shown at the train station where Edwinna and Elaine were to board the train to Des Moines to return to duty after being home for a week. *(Submitted by Elaine Homan)*

Flying lessons, anyone?

Gene Shank, left, and Bert McMahon gave pilot training at the airport in the 1930s. This photo, taken by O.T. "Tody" Jaynes in July of 1930, shows the men in front of a "Swallow" airplane. Bert managed the airport in 1930. *(Submitted by Robert Jaynes)*

A centennial event

Roger Hogey and his sister Margaret posed for this centennial photo in 1954. Roger entered the whisker growing contest. *(Submitted by Lorraine O'Learey)*

71

Canvas capers

This photo, taken around 1916 or 1917, shows a Mr. Bleds, an employee of the Sioux City Tent and Awning Company at 308-310 Jackson St. E.J. Wallen was the proprietor and the firm sold tents, cots and bedding and provided rentals. They could also make to order any canvas goods. Their motto was, "Not always the cheapest, but always the best." *(Submitted by Jack Rush)*

Sioux City slugger

Cornelius "Cal" Henry Callahan loved baseball and it shows in this early 1900s photograph. He played shortstop and moved to Sioux City from Kansas City. *(Submitted by Margaret Duman, daughter of Cornelius Callahan)*

Pentecostal Church

Eunice Gray was the preacher at the
Pentecostal Church at 1727 Fifth St. in 1954.
*(Submitted by Betty Gray, daughter-in-law of
Eunice Gray)*

Getting the job done

Construction of the two Sioux City reservoirs was done in 1937 by the Clark
Brothers Construction Co., owned by Lyman, George, Harvey and Horace Clark.
The work was done by mules, Model L Chalmers, graders and an elevator plow.
Workers lived in camp-like villages. There were sleeping, cooking and dining
shacks and a commissary on the site. *(Submitted by Wayne Hamilton, Larry Clark
and Joan Clark Johnson)*

A public servant

Dennis Ambrose Murphy took care of many important issues for Sioux Cityans by
serving as commissioner of parks and public property. He was well-loved by the
community and appears not to have a care in the world as he reads his newspaper in his backyard at 3254 Jones St., in 1940. *(Submitted by Camilla Murphy,
daughter of Dennis Murphy)*

Movin' down the line

Carl "Dutch" Mummert, second from the left, was an engineer for Chicago Northwestern Railroad in 1915. He worked from the city's rail yards at 16th Street and Floyd Boulevard. *(Submitted by Lucille Spurlock)*

The local mercantile

Alexander Socknat owned and operated Socknat's General Merchandise located at 4008-4010 Morningside Ave. Drilling Pharmacy is now located there. Alex stands in front of his store in 1954. The store sold everything from nuts to ice cream for 79 cents a half gallon. It was open seven days a week until 11 p.m. *(Submitted by Joan Socknat Thurber)*

The Katz meow

Katz Drug Store was located at Fourth and Pierce streets in this 1950s photo. Katz was known for its fountain drinks. *(Submitted by Ron Millage Sr.)*

Up, up and away

Joseph and Mary Peterson, left, and friends were taken for a novelty balloon ride at the 1912 Interstate Fair in Riverview Park in Sioux City. The fairground was superimposed behind the fake balloon. *(Submitted by Donald Sappingfield, grandson of Joseph and Mary Peterson)*

Batter up

Standard Clothing Co., was located at 710-712 Fourth St. It sponsored a baseball team in 1923, which included Art Boettcher (first row, seventh player) who was its pitcher. *(Submitted by Ruth Blake, daughter of Art Boettcher)*

Built for speed

Hawkeye Trucks were built in Sioux City at 2700 Floyd Blvd. The trucks were made for local and national sales as shown in this 1920 photo. A 1 1/2-ton truck sold for $1,850; a 2-ton truck sold for $2,650 and a 3 1/2-ton truck was $3,700. *(Submitted by Ron Millage Sr.)*

Rally around

Sioux City veterans got together to march to Washington D.C., for their bonuses. Veterans of World War II received a bonus for serving in the war. *(Undated photo submitted by Donald Owings)*

Supply and demand

Mads P. Nielsen, far right, sold groceries at M.P. Nielsen Meat Market at 2025 Riverside Blvd., in 1910. He also lived in the upstairs area, where rooms were rented out nightly. Streetcars and horses would deliver the products. *(Submitted by Robert Johnson)*

It's a convoy

Members of the Siouxland Antique Car Club parade downtown on Fourth and Pierce streets in this 1957 photo. The club would meet the first Tuesday of every month. Members would also travel to other areas to show their cars. *(Submitted by Jim McSparran)*

Tri State Produce Co.

This is an aerial view of Tri State Produce Co. taken in the 1940s. Tri State was located at 505 S. Howard St., and processed produce and shipped it to local businesses. The company was owned by Philip and Reva Sherman. *(Submitted by James Sherman)*

Danny Thomas visits

Danny Thomas poses with members of the Sioux City Chamber of Commerce in September of 1960. Thomas was in Sioux City to attend a fund-raiser for the St. Jude's Children's Hospital. *(Submitted by Jim Yanney, second from the left)*

Alley cats

Members of the War Eagle Alleys bowling team bowled every Thursday night at War Eagle Alley located where the current First Federal Bank is. Members were front row from left, Jeannette Wright Carney, Barbara Goldberg and Elois Ewing Borschuk. Second row, Mable Wilson, Eileen Haefs and Helen Klein. 1950 photo. *(Submitted by Elois Borschuk)*

Mother's little helper

Eleanor Elaine Brown, 1, helps with the chores in 1941 at her home at 612 George St. *(Submitted by Jay Dowdy, nephew of Eleanor Brown)*

Having a ball
Jim and Do Yanney, left, with Mary and Art Ellis are out on the town at an Abu-Bekr Shrine Ball in 1965. *(Submitted by Jim Yanney)*

Dreamy opportunity
Shari Duff, Cindy Waitt, Norm Waitt Sr., (back), Pat Boone, Kathy Breyspraak and Dee Dee Klute pose in this 1966 photo. *(Submitted by Joan Waitt, wife of Norm Waitt Sr.)*

Grand parade

Members of the 168th Infantry march at the Interstate Fair held in Woodlawn Park in this early 1900s photo. The soldiers trained at Woodlawn Park. Woodlawn Park was later named Interstate Park, then Riverview Park. *(Submitted by Frances Van Rennes)*

Great Northern

Frank W. Clark, left, and Mr. Geelan were engineers with Great Northern Railway. They are shown in front of a train on retirement day in 1950. *(Submitted by Frances Van Rennes, daughter of Frank Clark)*

It does a body good

Cindy, Norm Jr., Marcia and Ted Waitt get ready for bed with a glass of milk in this 1963 photo taken at their home at 3644 Cheyenne Blvd. *(Submitted by Joan Waitt, mother of Cindy, Norm Jr., Marcia and Ted)*

Trick roundhouse

Railroad workers for Chicago, Milwaukee, St. Paul Railroad pose in this 1932 photo. They were members of No. 2 Trick Roundhouse. *(Submitted by Ed Tryon)*

Opening day

This is a 1950 aerial photograph of Sioux City. The day this photo was taken was the opening dedication ceremony of the Municipal Auditorium. *(Submitted by Pakeltis Estate)*

Waiting on parts

M & S Co., 717-719 Pearl St., was owned and operated by Myrtle Smith. Mrs. Smith founded the company in 1936 as a wholesale automotive parts and machine shop. Late 1940s photo. *(Submitted by Vickie Henrichsen)*

Koschine's cuisine

William Koschine's restaurant, 1017 Fourth St., was a family-run business for 25 years. This restaurant was located where the parking lot across from the Bluestem Restaurant is today. *(Submitted by Dwight Boetger)*

Life and liability

J. Watt Wooldridge Insurance Agency was working hard in 1922 at their office in the Insurance Exchange Building. You could purchase property and casualty, now known as liability, insurance. *(Submitted by Jeff Wooldridge)*

Let's swing

Dugan's Harmony Peddlers was a five-piece union orchestra in 1925. The weekends were the big dance nights and the Harmony Peddlers could be seen. Brownie Walters, at the piano, was a 19-year-old who played by ear only. *(Submitted by Elaine Anderson, daughter of Brownie Walters)*

Hail Mardi Gras

Mary Hale Britton and David J. Albert were presented as the 1960 monarchs of Mardi Gras at the 31st Annual Pre-Lenten Ball held at Shore Acres Ballroom. Their attendants were Nancy Deever and Jeff Wooldridge. *(Submitted by Jeff Wooldridge)*

Roy, Dale and Trigger

Joan and Jack Freeman took a pony ride in 1941. A gentleman would go around to neighborhoods with his pony and give children rides and take their pictures for $1. *(Submitted by Malvina Guinther, mother of Joan and Jack)*

Just like new

This is Davenport Cleaners, 618-620 Pierce St., in 1938. Dean Collins, Cliff Omer, Frank Frohman, Lewis Dougherty and A.L. "Pete" Backus were the route men for the company. All you needed to do was call 55008. *(Submitted by Davenport Cleaners)*

Early to rise

Sophia Stanwick is taking the cow by the horns in this 1934 photo. Sophia and her sons could be seen at their home, 2512 Ridge Ave., doing chores. *(Submitted by Nancy Means, granddaughter-in-law of Sophia)*

Brains vs. brawn

In 1909, the Morningside College faculty played the senior baseball team. Members of the faculty were, from left, L.J. Griffith, athletic coach; R. Greynald, French; H.G. Campbell, philosophy; R.B. Wylie, biology; E. A. Brown, education; R.N. Van Horne, mathematics (behind the horse); unknown, W. L. Lewis, chemistry; F.H. Garver, history; and M.F. McDowell, physics. The faculty won the game. *(Submitted by Morningside College)*

Hi kids

Canyon Kid was an hour-long children's program seen on KVTV. Canyon Kid was played by Jim Henry and the show featured cartoons and special events from around Siouxland. *(Submitted by Jeff Wooldridge)*

War brides

With the advent of World War II, the ranks of married couples swelled in colleges and universities across the country. This 1945 scene at Morningside College was typical of those communities with active duty U.S. Army and Army Air Corps bases. From left, Mr. and Mrs. Fred Warner of Onawa, Iowa; Mr. and Mrs. Orin Goodrich (he was from Jefferson, Iowa, she was from Primghar, Iowa) and Mr. and Mrs. Norman Mutchler (He was from Sparta, Mich., she was from Sioux City). *(Submitted by Morningside College)*

Real man's game

In November 1917, Morningside College played Notre Dame in football at Mizzou Park in the Sioux City Stockyards. Face guards and other protective gear were unheard of in those days of football. *(Submitted by Morningside College)*

Helping the war effort

Morningside College was a training center for the war effort during World War II in 1945. Bass Field was the site for various drill and ceremonies performed by students training for duty at the college. *(Submitted by Morningside College)*

Clubbing around

This 1906 postcard shows the Riverside Boat Club located in Riverside Park. C.R. Marks was the president and W.R. Goudy was the secretary-treasurer. (*Submitted by Jim Oldenkamp*)

Now left, turn and bow

Evelyn Murray's Dance Studio was hopping in 1954. The studio, located at 615 1/2 Pierce St., was the scene of many spring recitals. *(Submitted by Terry Duzik)*

End of the line

George Churchill was a streetcar conductor in 1915. He served as a conductor for many years until moving to California. *(Submitted by Clarice Ryden, granddaughter of George Churchill)*

Kicking back

Sammy, Betty and Carolyn Scott enjoyed a nice summer day relaxing on the front lawn in this 1944 photo. *(Submitted by Betty Scott Gray)*

Hay-day

Daughters of Henry Clinton Crooks enjoyed a hayride with friends in this 1912 photo. Third from the left is Gertrude Heitritter Crooks, fourth, Josephine Francis Crooks, fifth, Bertha Maxfield Crooks and sixth, Bessie Martin Crooks. The Crooks farm is the current Whispering Creek Golf Course. *(Submitted by Joyce Maxfield)*

Home on leave

Edward Newman, right, visits with an unidentified man while home on leave from World War II in this 1940s photograph. Photo was taken on West 17th Street near the location of today's Applebee's. *(Submitted by Delores Weaver)*

Elmwood

The hall at the Elmwood, shown in this 1890 photo, located on Floyd Boulevard in Leeds welcomed many visitors. Norm Waitt purchased the Elmwood after it had been a nursing home and made it into a restaurant. *(Submitted by Joan Waitt)*

Off to the races

William Dorr, left, and his friend would go out to Riverside Park, where they had car races in 1929.
(Submitted by Lucille Spurlock)

Lend a helping hand.

The Floyd River flood of 1891 left many people in need of help from their neighbors. *(Submitted by Ed Tryon)*

Grave of a chief

This is the original resting place of Chief War Eagle as it looked in 1956. The grave site is located on the bluff overlooking I-29 and the Missouri and Big Sioux rivers. The grave was moved further from the edge of the bluff in 1989 when it began sloughing off and exposed some of the remains. A statue depicting War Eagle extending a peace pipe was erected in 1975 as a tribute to the man who befriended white settlers in what became Sioux City. *(Submitted by Sandra Lynch)*

The scholar

Joe Karpuk was a first grader in this 1928 photograph. He was a student at St. Frances Catholic School. *(Submitted by Joe Karpuk)*

Same as always

Green Gables, 1800 Pierce St., hasn't changed much since 1941. From the outside of the building to the hot fudge sundaes served inside, much remains the same. *(Submitted by Pakeltis Estate)*

Haulin' beef

Ray Cowan, cattle and machinery auctioneer, stands in front of his truck which he purchased from C. H. Condon in 1947 for approximately $5,000. The truck is attached to a Fruehauf trailer used for hauling live-stock. Photo was taken at Cowan's home north of Leeds in 1947. *(Submitted by Chuck Condon)*

Cruisin'

Chet Strong, Stan Greigg and Robert "Bob" Greigg were cruisin' on their doodle bugs in 1947 near the Greigg home at 1309 Morningside Ave. *(Submitted by David Greigg, son of Robert Greigg)*

A break in the war

Eugene McArthur, center, is home on leave during World War II and takes time to pose with his parents, Edith and Nathaniel McArthur in this 1943 photo. *(Submitted by Dorothy McArthur)*

Grand procession

Family members of Mrs. John Holdenreid enjoyed a buggy ride in front of the City Hall at Sixth and Douglas streets in this late 1800s photo. *(Susbmitted by Frances Sulzbach)*

Brothers three

The three McArthur brothers, Nathaniel, top, Lloyd, front, and Earl, middle, posed for this photo sometime between 1920 and 1925. Nathaniel worked for the Great Northern Railway company. Lloyd started the McArthur Sheet Metal business in 1934 and moved it to South Sioux City in 1952. Earl was a boxer and ranked third among the world's bantamweight contenders. *(Submitted by Dorothy McArthur)*

Hot dog

Milwaukee Lunch, located at 404 Fourth St., in 1937 was owned by Gus Avlichos for more than 20 years. Before his retirement, Gus recalled the record consumption in one sitting at his establishment was 68 hot dogs and 28 bottles of pop set by a returning World War II serviceman. John Diavastes, shown third from the right, was employed at Milwaukee Lunch for a couple of years. He made $1 per day and hot dogs sold for 5 cents each. *(Submitted by Georgia Diavastes, wife of John Diavastes)*

Fruits, vegetables for sale

Perazzo Confectionery, 901 Fourth St., sold fruits, vegetables and tobacco in the early 1920s. A soda fountain was also popular with customers. The business was owned and operated by Frank Perazzo. *(Submitted by Evelyn Perazzo Alvey, daughter of Frank Perazzo)*

All under control

This is Whittier School, Cedar Street and Fourth Avenue, in 1871. Dorothea Korstad Kroll stands in front of the sand box that these kindergarten students played in. *(Submitted by Dorothea Korstad Kroll)*

Tragedy at Swift

In 1949 there was an explosion at Swift and Co., packing plant which killed 20 people. One of them was Andrew Wisner who was working at the basement level when the explosion occurred. His wife Edna was working on the third level and helped other workers escape the building. *(Submitted by Sandy Parks, daughter of Andrew Wisner)*

It's over our head

Elaborated Ready Roofing Co., was located at 517 1/2 Nebraska St. Second from the left is Walter Lenz, who worked for the company for five years. Elaborated offered a five-year guarantee on materials and workmanship. Its payment plan policy was one year to pay without interest. 1931 photo. *(Submitted by Pat Duff, daughter of Walter Lenz)*

Front yard monster

Lori, 5, dressed as a leopard, and Cindy Duff, 7, dressed as Batman, get ready for Halloween in 1966. The girls wanted to make a monster in their front yard at 3319 Virginia St., and this scarecrow is what they came up with. *(Submitted by Pat Duff, mother of Lori and Cindy)*

When things heat up

George Sheets served four years with the Sioux City Fire Department, inaugurating the motor equipment. This was the first fire chief car for George Kellogg and Sheets was his driver. This 1914 photo was taken in front of the Hose and Ladder Company No. 1 at 408 Water St. *(Submitted by Phyllis and Vern Fleck)*

Attention!

Henry, left, and Miles Klosterman are shown in this Christmas 1942 photo. They received play military outfits. *(Submitted by Deanna Klosterman, wife of Miles Klosterman)*

Ladies and gents

Ralph E. Ricker Jr., delivers the Ladies Home Journal in 1928. The photo was taken at 1516 Ross St. Ralph is ready to go to work in his tie and knickers. *(Submitted by Susan Fracisco, granddaughter of Ralph E. Ricker Jr.)*

Learning their three Rs

This is how a classroom looked about 1900 at Hawthorne School. Students are still being taught in this classroom today. The school is located at 4405 Central St. *(Submitted by Lola Brown)*

Early Leeds business

This is the Rich Bros. Coal, Wood & Feed store at 917 Floyd Ave., in Leeds. Photo was taken in 1910. Owners were Charles J. Rich and William E. Rich. *(Submitted by Lola Brown)*

101

Young ladies club

Members of the MYOB, an all-girls club founded by Mrs. Beulah Webb, are shown with their dates for a special evening of dancing. The girls invited their escorts to the dance with a formal invitation. The photo was taken around 1940 in the social room above Roberts Dairy Co. Inc., 114 W. 14th St. *(Submitted by Laura Harrison)*

Masters of the hoops

This is the basketball team sponsored by the Tolerton & Warfield Co., (Council Oak Stores) in the 1931-32 season. Front row from left are Ray Rye, Harold Storm, Willis Link and Marvin Rickman. Standing from left are team manager Lymer, M. Clark, Virgil Moore and Allen Pettit. *(Submitted by Donna Goehring)*

Boxing robe fitting

Quill Hoberg, left, was a member of the Bob Burns boxing team in 1943 representing the Airborne 101 Division. Dwight Hauff, right, provided uniforms for the team. The photo was taken at Hauff Sporting Goods store. *(Submitted by Dwight Hauff)*

Major league future

Johnny Niggeling, left, and Soos' manager Joe Becker posed for this photograph in 1947 at Soo's Ball Park. Niggeling was a knuckle ball pitcher who went on to a major league career. He made his debut with the Washington Senators. *(Submitted by Dwight Hauff)*

Miss USO

An airman congratulates Laura Carter Harrison after it was announced at a dance at the Sioux City air base around 1943 that she had been voted Miss USO by the servicemen. Miss WAC is at right but is unidentified. *(Submitted by Laura Carter Harrison)*

A church gathering

The congregation of the Old Mount Zion Church, Sixth and Bluff streets, gathers for a group photo on a Sunday morning in 1914 or 1915. At the far right, wearing the black top hat, is the Rev. Herbit, pastor of the congregation. *(Submitted by Laura Harrison)*

Dime store hoppin'

Delores Whitlock, 4, left, and Donna Whitlock, 3, are shopping in downtown Sioux City in 1950 with their mother Marge Whitlock. *(Submitted by Donna Whitlock)*

Preparing for the fights

Bill Enockson, left, and Walt Case, employees of Hauff's Sporting Goods, model the new jackets to be worn by the boxers who participated in the 1952 Golden Gloves tournament, sponsored by the Journal-Tribune. The event was held in the Municipal Auditorium. Photo was taken at Hauff Sporting Goods store. *(Submitted by Dwight Hauff)*

Relay workout

This is the 1945 medley relay team for the Trinity Crusaders. From left are John Dougherty, Bob McDougal, Tom Donohue and Connie Callahan. The boys were working out prior to the state track meet. Their coach was Vince McMahan. *(Submitted by Dwight Hauff)*

Hi, ref

Doug Bragdon is shown in this 1930s photo refereeing a high school football game. Bragdon was a Sioux City athletic official for 30 years. *(Submitted by Dwight Hauff)*

Busy day at the West

Convention goers gather outside the West Hotel in June of 1912. The hotel was located at the northwest corner of Third and Nebraska streets. *(Submitted by Dave Gordon)*

Cigar inventory

Harry S. Zanfes was owner of Harry's Cafe (also known as Harry's Hamburgers) at 719 Fourth St. In this early 1960s photo, Harry takes inventory of the cafe's specialty cigars which can also be seen in the photo. *(Submitted by Marty Bostinelos)*

A class portrait

Members of the second grade at Lowell school, 1801 27th St., gathered for this photo in 1956. Front row from left are Dorothy Kerns, Pamela DeLashmut, Linda Johnson, Sharon Smith, Janet Swinford, Kathy DeMary, unidentified, unidentified. Second row from left are Juanita Plinket, unidentified, Barbara Strike, Ray Patten, John Hines, unidentified, unidentified, Ernest Thurston, unidentified. Back row from left, Miss Thompson (teacher), unidentified, John Satler, unidentified, Howard Karras, unidentified, unidentified, Don Prath, unidentified. *(Submitted by Alfred Smith)*

Sioux City 'Field of Dreams'

The Sioux City Cornhuskers shown on this 1916 postcard won what was advertised as the world series of 1891 by defeating the Chicago White Stockings, National League champions. The Sioux City team won four out of six games at Evans Park. The "Huskers," as the team was better known, held the Western Association pennant, edging out Kansas City. *(Submitted by Frances Peterson)*

Their wedding day

Herbert "Hibby" Spencer and Vivian Bristow were married June 12, 1925, and posed for this photograph. The marriage took place at 1802 Center St.,, in the house where Vivian was born in 1906. *(Submitted by Marge Camp)*

Toe-tappin' femme fatales

In this 1918 photo, members of the Judson Girls Orchestra prepare for another private party performance. The band was led by Miss Tess Quigley who is not shown. From left are Martha Metz (saxophone), Marian Lowe (trumpet) Gertrude White (violin), Grace Howe (piano) and Sarah Halverson Haller (drums, bells, xylophone and chimes). The popular all-female group performed at many private parties throughout the city. *(Submitted by Sally Haller Oswald, daughter of Sarah Halverson Haller)*

Sweet deal

Pearl, Ray and Mark DeForce are pictured in Pearl's Candy Store located at 509 Pearl St., in this 1915 photo. Pearl started the business at age 25 with an eighth grade education. She took some correspondence courses, then started the business. She owned and operated the store from 1915 to 1925. The store also had a messenger service. *(Submitted by Frances Heuertz)*

Shoeing the horseless carriage

This is an interior view of the Haller Brothers Tire Shop at 428 Douglas St., in 1922. This was the firm's second location. The business originated at 413 Pearl St., in about 1916. At right is the owner, John Haller. The firm handled Fisk, Michelin and Kelly Springfield tires. Occasionally, Haller's wife, Sara Halverson Haller, would come down to the shop and run the cash register. *(Submitted by Sally Haller Oswald)*

Davidson Bros. Co. employees

Davidson Bros. Co., located on Fourth and Pierce streets, was a well-known department store. This 1936 photo shows the employees who kept the company going. *(Submitted by Pat Mustain)*

Tricycle built for two

Walter, 4, and Wilbur, 3, Lefler enjoyed a day playing at what's now Kelly Park in this 1921 photo. The photo was taken on Wilbur's birthday. The Leflers attended church that day and had the family over for dinner. *(Submitted by Theresa Gray)*

Care to read with us?

Carl Engstrand, left, James Engstrand and an unidentified boy read the newspaper in this 1916 photo taken at 410 Rebecca St. Could their newspaper be the Sioux City Journal? *(Submitted by Margaret Engstrand, sister of Carl and James Engstrand)*

Tea, coffee and everything nice

The Excel Tea Co., 511 Pearl St., was owned and operated by Afa S. Harris. Harris is shown standing beside his delivery truck in 1931. He often traveled to Europe to purchase his tea. He also sold coffee and spices. *(Submitted by Joe Oddo)*

Discipline, discipline, discipline

D.D. Zinn, right, principal of Hopkins School, 916 W. Eighth St., appears to be reprimanding Danny Desmond, custodian, in this 1949 gag photo. *(Submitted by Donna Fritch Fuller)*

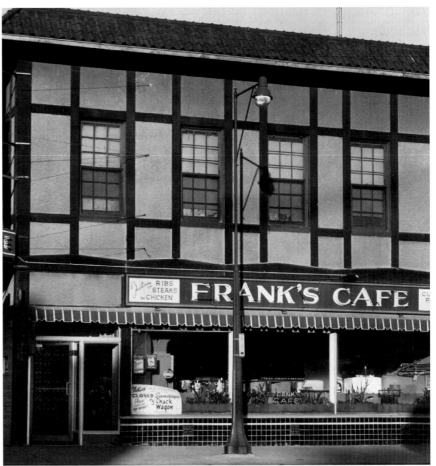

Order please

Helen and Frank Kahoun owned and operated Frank's Cafe located at 624 Pierce St. The cafe served ribs, chicken and steak. Its hours were 6 a.m. to 2 a.m., Monday through Saturday. Photo taken in 1955. *(Submitted by Helen Kahoun)*

Wash and set

The Sioux City Beauty Academy was located on the second floor at 517 Fourth St., in 1937. The academy was owned and operated by Rachel Kahoun. Many people would go to the school to have their hair done. *(Submitted by Helen Kahoun, daughter-in-law of Rachel Kahoun)*

Sunbeam Lady visits

The Sunbeam Appliance Lady is welcomed to Sioux City in 1960 by M.W. "Bud" Torrey, left, general manager of Warren Electric Co., and Rudy Schindler, owner of Schindler's Jewelry store and a member of the welcoming committee. Warren Electric Co., was founded in 1919 by G.R. Warren, George Wissing and Roger Carlson with an initial $2,500 investment. Today, the firm has grown into a multi-million dollar operation with headquarters in Houston with 34 other locations in the United States and four in foreign countries. *(Submitted by Nancy Harrington-Torrey, wife of "Bud" Torrey)*

Bring on the music

The 10th Annual Iowa Bandmasters Convention was held in Sioux City June 6, 7 and 8, 1937. This photo was taken at the Sioux City bandshell in Grandview Park. Pictured from left are, Leo Kucincski, 1937 president and host of the convention, Conrad Claussen, Milburn McKay, George W. Landers, James Melichar, Mose Reed, Karl King, Glen L. Lyman and Alonzo Leach. The Iowa Bandmasters program included concerts, clinics, demonstrations and reviews of new music, election of officers for the coming year and a banquet. *(Submitted by George Burg)*

It's a girl thing

Dorothy, Maxine, Eleanor and Edith McArthur clown around in this 1929 photo. It looks as if Billy McArthur is feeling a little left out. *(Submitted by Dorothy McArthur)*

Dancing darling

Marilyn Brown Tyler takes a few moments to pose gracefully for this 1945 ballet photo taken at 1615 West St. Marilyn took ballet lessons for many years and was on her way to a dance recital when the photo was taken. *(Submitted by Cindy McDole, niece of Marilyn Brown Tyler)*

Beep-beep

Dickson-Hoak sold new Dodge and Plymouth cars as well as used cars at 219 W. Seventh St. Lloyd LaFleur, shown in this late 1940s early 1950s photo, was one of their salesmen. He later opened LaFleur Pontiac in 1960. *(Submitted by Cindie Pedersen, daughter of Lloyd LaFleur)*

117

Banking on its employees

Employees of the Livestock National Bank are shown in this 1921 photo. They are from left, Bill Schenk, Merle Kempton, Raws Jensen, Clifford Adams, Mark Wilson, Happy Olson, Ivan Holmberg, Carroll Philips, Mildred Lenagh, Shorty Scharles, Helen Saldonias, Margaret Fallon, Abe Brunich, Irene Nomsen, Harvey Scott, Cliff Boyer and Bill Nelson. *(Submitted by Larry Fuller, son of Irene Nomsen)*

Having a ball

Winters in Sioux City are the perfect time to have an old-fashioned snowball fight. In 1946, it looks as if Joyce Coyle and her friend Myra Fitzgerald were preparing for just that. Myra's brother, Doug Fitzgerald, has other ideas of what a snowball fight is. *(Submitted by Mark and Ellen Ayers)*

Men in black

Desk sergeants George E. Peirce, left, and Platt H. Ford seem to be talking about some interesting case in this December 1906 photo. Both were part of the police staff and helped keep law and order in Sioux City. *(Submitted by Joe Stabile)*

The one that got away

Ron Lenz, left, is getting some dryland fishing tips from his big brother, Walter Lenz, in this 1936 photo taken at 215 S. Linn St. The boys wanted to go fishing, but all they had was a stick and string. *(Submitted by Ron Lenz)*

Another day at the office

In 1949, D.K. Baxter Co., was a busy wholesale distributor of Frigidaire refrigerators, electric ranges and many other home appliances. The company was established in 1924 and was located at 806 Pierce St. From left are Mary Louise Mills, accounts payable; Phyllis Haller Bergstrom, secretary; Donald D. Sappingfield, accounts receivables; Kathleen Malloy Flynn, receptionist; John F. Fieselman, office manager; Donald E. Wilson, bookkeeping; Harold H. Boe, accounting and payroll; Frank Slavec, assistant credit manager, and Catherine Magirl Tott, posting machine operator. *(Submitted by Donald Sappingfield)*

Ace up your sleeve

This photo, taken around 1914, shows Sioux City patrolmen taking time out for a card game. From left are Ed Rath, Bill Mertz, Bill Hatch, Blondie Barker, Ed Kirby and Police Chief Michael O'Shonessy. O'Shonessy served as police chief from 1914 to 1916. *(Submitted by Bev Walding)*

Just a little H2O

A 1953 science class at Briar Cliff College. *(Submitted by Briar Cliff College)*

Bonnet beauties

In 1915, these seven young ladies would frequently picnic at Grace Grove, which is today's Bacon Creek Park. They would pack a lunch and walk a mile to their picnic spot. While there they played ball and other games and then they would sing their way home. From left are Alice Kendall, Faye Holloway, Mary Cummins, Mary Kirby, Anna Dahl, Ethel Nystrom and Edna O'Shonessy Walding. *(Submitted by Bev Walding, daughter of Edna O'Shonessy Walding)*

Free rides

John F. McLeod, front, and Giles Tuttle, on the patrol wagon, look as if they are ready to capture a fugitive in this 1907 photo. They were on the police staff protecting and serving the community. *(Submitted by Joe Stabile)*

Walking shoes

Hanna's Shoe Repair, shown in this 1931 photo, was located at 719 1/2 Pierce St. Hanna's grand opening was June 1, 1931. Owner Jim Hanna, right, and his sister Julia Hanna, left, worked many hours repairing, dyeing and shining shoes. There were days Jim Hanna would work from 7 a.m. to midnight because he had problems finding staff. *(Submitted by Jim Hanna)*

People of manufacturing

Employees of Sioux City Battery Co., gather outside of their building for this 1954 photo. The company was located at 323 Water St., and employed many people. This photo was taken just after the Korean war, a time when many women were entering the workforce. *(Submitted by Donald Sappingfield)*

Truckin' trike

Jim Brown smiles as he rides his tricycle in 1945 while taking a break during his play time. Jim is now an independent truck driver. *(Submitted by Cindy McDole, niece of Jim Brown)*

Lights out

The Cudahy Packing Co. located at 900 S. Chambers St., covered 23 acres and was one of Sioux City's major meat packers. The plant was closed in October 1954. This 1930 photo shows the electrical staff, better known as the "electrical gang." The men handled all the electrical aspects of the plant. *(Submitted by the children of Oscar Olson)*

Full steam ahead

The last smoker train passes through Riverside as it enters Sioux City July 1, 1952. It was the end of a proud era for the old steam locomotives in Sioux City. *(Submitted by Joe Oddo)*

No ballgame today

The 1953 Floyd River flood innundated the Soos' ballpark located near Leeds. The rains began early Sunday morning June 7 and continued throughout the day washing out the scheduled game between the Soos and the Denver Bears that evening. Heaviest rainfall was in the northern reaches of the Floyd River valley where some areas recorded as much as 11 inches. Sioux City was hit by surprise about 10 a.m. Monday by a wall of water slamming into the city. It was Sioux City's worst disaster, causing the loss of 14 lives and more than $23 million in damages. *(Submitted by Bob Humphrey)*

Giddy up, nanny

Lucille Mummert Spurlock and Lois Mummert Beers enjoy a goat cart ride in this 1915 photograph. The owner of the goat cart would travel throughout Sioux City and offer kids rides and a picture for around 5 cents. The photo was taken at the girls' home at 16th and Court streets. *(Submitted by Lucille Spurlock)*

And baby makes three

This family photo was taken in 1931 of Lewis A. Huber, his daughter Dorothy H. Huber and his wife Helen C. Huber.
(Submitted by Dorothy McArthur)

Celebrating Christmas

Employees of the Livestock National Bank are shown at their 1943 Christmas party. The bank was located at the Exchange Building at the stockyards. Zita Galvin sang a couple of Christmas solos for the occasion.
(Submitted by Zita Galvin)

Too cool for my own good

With no air conditioning in 1954, Mary Anderson Semple took the cool way out. It's hard to believe this little one now works in the circulation department for the Sioux City Journal. *(Submitted by Mary Jane Anderson)*

See baby see

Dorothy Terpenning Bos, 2 1/2, left, and Ruth Boettcher Blake, 4, hold their baby dolls on the steps of the Floyd Monument in this 1929 photo. *(Submitted by Ruth Blake)*

At the links

These golfers pose before an exhibition game for a photo about 1950 at the Sioux City Boat Club course. Front row from left are Jimmy Thomson, Bill Adams (Boat Club pro), Horton Smith, Johnny Goodman. Back row from left are Joe Weir, unknown, Bill Hogen and unknown. *(Submitted by Dwight Hauff)*

Have bike will deliver

Mark, Ray and Pearl DeForce stand in front of Pearl's messenger company in this 1915 photo. The messenger company was located at 509 Pearl St. Pearl also owned a candy store in the same building. Mark and Ray would deliver packages, mail and Western Union messages. Pearl operated the business from 1915 to 1925. *(Submitted by Frances Heuertz)*

Rah rah, sis boom bah

Cathy Wilen poses in this 1969 photo at 2823 Myrtle St. Cathy was a football cheerleader for Central High School from 1969 to 1970. *(Submitted by Cathy Wilen Podwysocki)*

Just chillin'

The Penguin Ice Cream Shop in Cecila Park was a favorite hangout for the guys in 1950. Pictured are, top to bottom, John Overstreet, Niel Mischo, Tom J. O'Connor and Charles Maskovich. In the background is the owner, Henry Lauson. *(Submitted by Ron Lenz)*

A fair estimation

Joe Morten, left, Laura Morten, sister, and Al Burling are at the Dakota County Fair. They gave fairgoers a glimpse of what their business was doing in this 1940 photo. *(Submitted by Great West Casualty)*

Tough regimen

In 1944, the nurses at St. Joseph's School of Nursing attended roll call at 6 a.m., went to Mass, then were on duty by 7 a.m. They would also attend classes from 9 a.m. to 3 p.m. Because of World War II, nurses were in short supply so students would often work longer shifts at St. Joseph's Hospital. Pictured are Marge Fitzpatrick, unknown, unknown, Patty Mann, unknown, unknown, and Mary Jane Sheehan. *(Submitted by Mary Jane Anderson)*

129

Movin down the road

Council Oak Grocery Stores used trucks to deliver their goods throughout Sioux City. The trucks belonged to Holdcrest Trucking and were insured by Joe Morten and Son Insurance Agency. *(1950 photo, submitted by Great West Casualty)*

America's favorite pastime

Can you image a summer without America's favorite pastime? Little league baseball was played at Pulaski Park off Highway 75 in this 1962 photo. *(Submitted by Michael Furlich)*

130

Aren't you done yet?

Douglas Furlich seems bored with the idea of getting a haircut in this 1960 photo. Neighbor Romain Richardson cut Douglas' hair about once a month. *(Submitted by Douglas' father, Michael Furlich)*

Catching some rays

Nurses from St. Joseph's School of Nursing enjoy some sun in this 1944/1945 photograph. Between their shifts and classes, the gals would try to relax by going up on the roof of St. Joseph's Nursing Home. *(Submitted by Mary Jane Anderson)*

Kissing cousins

Margaret Olson and Marian St. Onge give each other a little kiss in front of the Floyd Monument in this 1931 photo. Both girls were 2 years old, and still remain close friends. *(Submitted by Margaret Gill)*

Bekins Van and Storage Co.

John Bekins was president of the company and Paul Bekins was vice president. Bekin's offered storage for household goods, autos and merchandise. This 1934 photo shows their building at Third and Douglas. *(Submitted by Pat Mustain)*

Sharing means caring

Mark Griggs, 3, offers his cousin, Douglas Furlich, 4, a bite of his cookie, even though Douglas already has a cookie. *(1959 photo submitted by Douglas' father, Michael Furlich)*

Grandpa time

Charles "Chuck" Clayton Torrey mugs the camera along the river bank in this 1938 photo with his grandfather David Torrey. The two were taking a break from the daily grind and spending some quality time along the Missouri River. *(Submitted by Nancy Harrington Torrey)*

One man's trash

Is another mans treasure, but for Mr. Metcalf and Pat Alvarez the day was not that lucky in this late 1960s photo taken at the landfill. *(Submitted by Pat's mother, Elvira Alvarez)*

What might have been

This artist's rendition shows what the Woodbury County Courthouse may have looked like in the 1910s, without the City Hall to the south. *(Submitted by Bob Knowler)*

And the band played on

The Sioux City Recreational Band played at many school functions, parks and just for fun. The band was started by word of mouth and all members were volunteers. In this 1953 photo, the band was on its way to another performance. *(Submitted by Elvira Alvarez)*

The real McCoy

McCoy's Pharmacy, located at 1501 W. Third St., was owned and operated by John J. McCoy from 1918 to 1944. The pharmacy had a big soda fountain. John had 11 children and everyone helped out at the pharmacy all the way down to delivering the medicine to the customers. 1922 photo. *(Submitted by John McCoy)*

Hi-ho and away

Harry and Edna Emery are on their way for a Sunday ride from their home near Leeds known then as Fair Acres in this 1928 photo. *(Submitted by Blanche Oslin, their grandaughter)*

Ho-ho-ho

Barb Baker, left, stopped by the home of her cousins, Cindy and Ellen Baker at 3416 Virginia St. early on Christmas morning to see the new bundle of joy they received. Santa delivered Blackie to Cindy and Ellen while they were sleeping. *(1960 photo submitted by Ellen Baker Ayers)*

Peg's tap

Peg's Tavern was located at 714 Fourth St. If you stopped at Peg's you would be greeted with a cold beer and a smile from bartender Dorothy Crowther in the early 1940s. *(Submitted by Ellen Ayers)*

Pipe dreams

Plumbers from Union 33 of Sioux City were employed by V.J. Hagan Co., to do the plumbing in the new St. Joseph's Hospital, 23rd and Court streets, in this 1951 photo. The old St. Joseph Hospital was built in 1890. *(Submitted by Pat Lowndes, husband Bob is pictured seventh from the left)*

137

First grads

This is the first graduating class from Leeds High School in 1941. First row, from left, Jenette Speckman, Alice DeWall, Joy Mead, Shirley Holt, Agatha Kellogg, Margaret Dreves and LaVerne Taute. Second row, Mr. S.M. Hickman (principal), Don Harward, Edna Mae Nelson, Valma Mae Laydu, Ruth Peterson, Marguerite Deuschle, Marilyn Mote, Zella Mae Vermilyea, Lucyle Zentz, Miss Helen Herrling, Ralph Junck and J. Neil Raudabaugh. Third row, Albert Priebe, Everett Hooks, Eugene McArthur, Jack Smith, Warren Riediger, Lake Kellogg, Ernest Mevius, Paul Conway, Paul Crame and Harry Shellenberger. *(Submitted by Dorothy McArthur)*

Slide for life

This 1927 picture was taken on the playground at Hobson Elementary School at 222 S. Wall St. In front is Andrew Rojas and behind him is his sister, Elvira Rojas Alvarez. *(Submitted by Elvira Alvarez)*

You don't say

Little Regina McArthur Hanna looks totally captivated by the conversation in this 1949 photo. *(Submitted by Dorothy McArthur)*

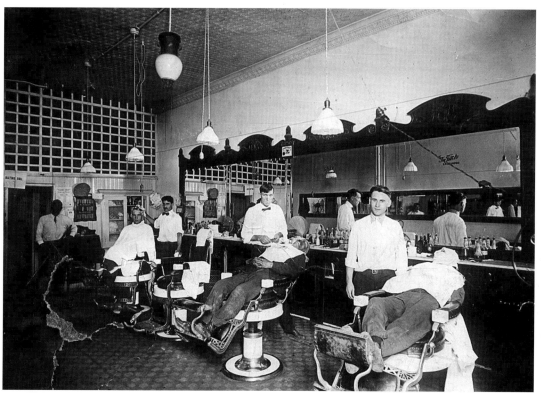

Classic cut

Owner and main barber Ellis Hanna, third from left, shampoos a customer in this photo taken around 1911. Ellis named his barber shop "Monarch." The shop, located on Fourth Street between Iowa and Wall streets, offered many services including baths, hair washes, massages, shaves and haircuts. Customers would pay fifty cents for a bath because many hotels did not have bath houses. *(Submitted by Jim Hanna, son of Ellis Hanna)*

Rock of education

Dorothy M. Huber sits on a rock in front of Central High School in this 1946 photo. *(Submitted by Dorothy McArthur)*

Insure them all

Joe W. Morten stands in front of his insurance business at 20th Street and Dakota Ave. in South Sioux City (the State Theatre Building) in this 1940 photo. Morten insured trucking businesses in the area. *(Submitted by Great West Casualty)*

Chief cook, bottle washer

Marie "Peewee" Westendorf works the counter at War Eagle Bowling Alley, 521 Pierce St., in 1951. She waitressed and cooked there for 35 years. She prepared all food from scratch. One of the more popular dishes was her chicken noodle soup with home-made noodles. The lunch counter was a favorite lunch spot of Journal employees. *(Submitted by Helen Miller, daughter of Marie Westendorf)*

Employees put the call out

Employees of Joe Morten Insurance Agency, in this mid 1950s photo, would call insured customers as well as take calls. The office only had four phone lines available at its 24th Street and Dakota Avenue office in South Sioux City. *(Submitted by Great West Casualty)*

Beefing up

Courier Holman, left, and Andy Anderson are pictured in front of the IBP Dakota City plant in this 1966 photograph. The two founded Iowa Beef Packers in 1960 and were responsible for many revolutionary changes in the beef packing industry. *(Submitted by IBP inc.)*

Morningside editors

Morningside College's board of editors are shown in 1901. From left are Editor-in-Chief Florence M. Cate of Correctionville, Iowa; Assistant Editor Ross P. Brown; Calendar, Bessie M. Carr; Literary Editor Chas F. Eberly; Faculty Ethel M. Walker; Business Manager Guy G.F. Frary; Literary Editor Emma A. Flathers; Assistant Manager Samuel Knoer and Literary Editor Ethel Gantt, all of Sioux City. *(Submitted by Debra Eberly)*

Greenberg Jewelry

Greenberg Jewelry located at 821 4th St., now the Sioux City Convention Center, is shown in this late 1920s or early 1930s photo. Pictured are second from the left, Jacob Greenberg, Miles Bradbury (watchmaker), unknown, women lady customers, Harry Johnson (bookkeeper) and Joseph H. Bolstein (salesman). Joseph H. Bolstein and Jacob Greenberg co-owned the building. Jacob Greenberg owned and operated the company. *(Submitted by Ray Greenberg)*

Family photo

This is a 1925 photograph of the Waitt family. Front row from left are Mary Lou Waitt, unidentified, Jean Waitt and the rest unidentified. Middle row are unidentified, unidentified, Ella Holman Waitt, George Waitt and others unidentified. Back row are Burt Waitt, Betty Waitt, Holman Waitt, Hazel Waitt, Clara Waitt, Cap Waitt, next three unidentified, Lucy Waitt, Katherine Waitt and Theodore Waitt. This photo was taken during the 50th anniversary of Ella Holman Waitt and George Waitt. *(Submitted by Norman Waitt Sr.)*

Before Wells Fargo

The Lewis System is what Wells Fargo was called back in the late 1930s and 1940s. This photograph was taken in the mid 1940s. In center, front row is Merrell Ray Sardeson. *(Submitted by Jay Dawdy, great-grandson of Sardeson)*

Making dough

Habooba Hanna of 4321 Fourth Ave., would bake bread for 13 people as shown in this 1940s photo. The loaves of flat bread would be two feet wide and be stacked two feet high. She would bake about a 150 loaves a week. *(Submitted by Jim Hanna, son of Habooba Hanna)*

The one that didn't get away

Glenn Musselman of Leeds High School grasps the football while trying to break the hold of Sonny Thacker of South Sioux City in this 1943 football game at the Leeds football field. Sonny did tackle Glenn. *(Submitted by Wendy Oldenkamp, daughter of Glenn Musselman)*

145

Step right up

If you stopped in at L. O'Harrow Shoe Store at 902 Fourth St., in 1901, you would find Len O'Harrow, Foster Thompson, Oscar Nystrom and Charlie Breum there to serve you. Before you entered the store, Jerry the horse would welcome you. *(Submitted by Adele Wood, granddaughter of Len O'Harrow)*

The crowning choice

June Archer, standing with Don Nissen, was crowned Miss A.I.B. by the Sioux City chapter of the American Institute of Banking in 1962. Miss Archer was employed with Morningside State Bank. *(Submitted by Ila Carlson)*

Leeds baseball

This is the Leeds baseball team in about 1940. At far right in the front row is Fred Utecht. Third from left, front row is Wayen Dirksen. Other players are not identified. *(Submitted by Ethelyn Knoernschild)*

Head up, shoulders back

Young ladies demonstrate proper posture at Briar Cliff College in the late 1940s. *(Submitted by Briar Cliff College)*

To the rescue

Members of the first Civil Defense Unit pose for this picture during the 1950s. *(Submitted by Ron Millage Sr.)*

Weights and measures

A Briar Cliff College chemistry class is being taught by Sister Mary Edward in the early 1960s. *(Submitted by Briar Cliff College)*

Tough guy pose

Glenn Fritch, left, Vic Reynolds and a man known as "Tarzan" pose in front of Glenn's car at their residence at 1617 W. Second St., in this 1935 or 1936 photograph. The three men rented the room from Alize Daniels. Glenn was the only one to have a car. *(Submitted by Donna Fuller, daughter of Fritch)*

Nightingales

Nurses at Samaritan Hospital, now known as St. Luke's Regional Medical Center, were expected to sweep floors, dust furniture, bring in coal and wash windows, as well as care for their patients. This group of Samaritan nurses in 1914 probably worked a 13-hour day. They were paid very little, perhaps $30 a month. Pictured are Grace Whitney, Signe Hammerlind, Erma Custer, Irene Dann, Madelon Box, Margaret McAthie and Agnes Moe. *(Submitted by St. Luke's Regional Medical Center)*

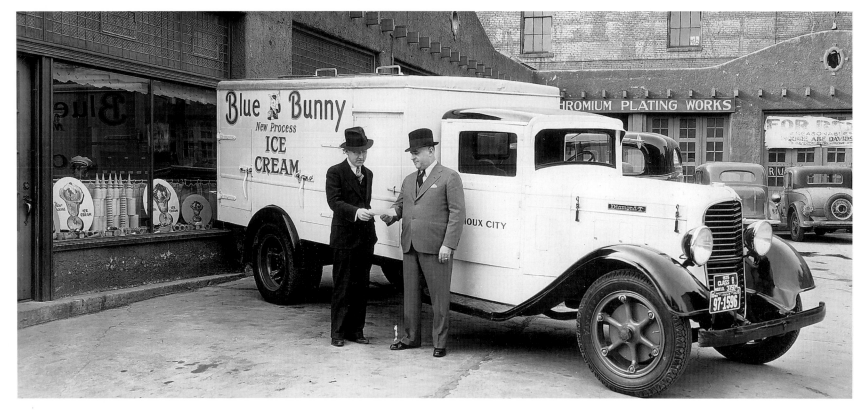

A winning combination

In 1927, Fred H. Wells and his brother, Harry C. Wells, began a partnership to distribute ice cream in Sioux City. A "Name That Ice Cream" contest was held in 1935. Harry C. Wells is pictured here presenting the $25 first prize to George Vanden Brink, Sioux City Journal artist, who came up with the winning name and the first logo, which appears on the ice cream truck behind the two men. *(Submitted by Wells Blue Bunny)*

Aim for the middle

Clair L. Blair takes aim in this 1948 photo. Clair was a student at Morningside College, where he majored in business. *(Submitted by Terry Duzik, daughter of Clair)*

Stepping out

Raymond T. Hopkinson, second from left, is stepping out with the Abu-Bekr Shrine Foot Patrol in this 1947 photo. Hopkinson was a former city councilman and active in politics. The photo was taken in the 600 block of Fifth Street. *(Submitted by Patricia Drommer Will)*

Me, me, me, meee

A choir group of Briar Cliff College students in the 1950s. *(Submitted by Briar Cliff College)*

Convention ready

Monahan Post No. 64 Official National American Legion Band poses in the late 1920s as it prepares for another convention. Before the band was named the Monahan Post Band, it was the Journal newsboy band. Prior to World War I, the forerunner of the Monahan Post Band was made up of Journal newsboy paper carriers. *(Submitted by Eleanor Tasker)*

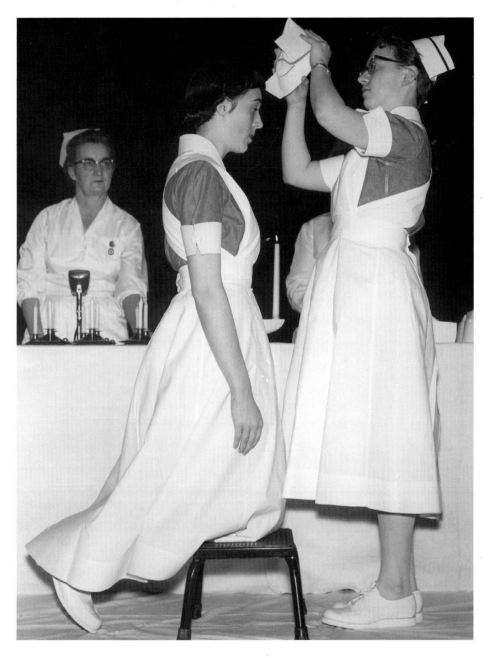

The capping

Student nurse Marlis J. Allen is capped in this 1957 photo. When a student nurse is "capped" she is definitely a member of the school. Marlis was a nurse for 36 years. The photo was taken at the Municipal Auditorium and Marlis attended Sioux City Methodist Hospital School of Nursing. *(Submitted by Viva Allen, mother of Marlis J. Allen)*

Head of the class

Joey Stark, Bev Miller, Cora Mattingly, Giny Searls, Dee Johnson, Tunky McMahon, Alex Fotis, Lois Foreman and Ramona Brouillette were mid-year graduates from Central High School in 1948. The graduates are pictured in Grandview Park. *(Submitted by Virginia Weaver)*

Need a delivery?

H.H. Polley owned and operated Polley's Grocery at 912 Plymouth St., now known as Highway 75. He would make two deliveries a day. If a customer forgot something, he would call Polley and he would make an extra run. Polley is photographed in this 1932 photo with his family, left to right, Dorothy Polley Ringsrud, Bonnie Polley Lake, Mr. Polley and Agnes Polley. *(Submitted by Bonnie Lake)*

Activity winner

Cliff Reppert is shown with his 1938 Harley Davidson motorcycle in this 1939 photo. He had won an activity contest for the most mileage and entering the most competitions. Every year a contest was held for entries in the most competitions. *(Submitted by Bud Albrecht)*

Harley buddies

The Soo Cycle Club was located on West Fourth Street near Riverside. The club had 45 to 50 members and would meet every Thursday. The Harley Davidson Indian motorcycles were the most popular bikes. In this 1950 photo, standing from left are, Cliff Reppert, Dorance Allen, Bill Lechner, Bob Morrow, unknown, Ted Alvey, Bob Schultz, Carl Noltze, Bud Albrecht, Ted Hayden, Dick DeLap and unknown. Front from left, Carl Olson, Art Olson, unknown, Lee Hackett, Jack Sandage, Johnny Beavers, Merrill Dillon, Bernard Whiting and Dan Pfaff. *(Submitted by Bud Albrecht)*

Westcott woes

The 1953 flood came to Sioux City and caused much devastation. Many bridges were destroyed including the Westcott Street bridge. *(Submitted by Eleanor Peterson)*

Exchange gals

All the women who worked at the Livestock Exchange Building posed for this 1954 photo. They were dressed up at work to celebrate the Sioux City centennial. *(Submitted by Geneva Stoltz Miller)*

It's all in the bait

Carl Petronis, 15, must have used the right bait to catch this 72-pound catfish in 1946. The photo was taken near where the Big Sioux joins the Missouri River, which is now I-29. *(Submitted by Mary Jo Petronis, wife of Carl Petronis)*

INDEX

Worst flood in years

In 1908 Perry Creek flooded in what was called the worst flood in years. Because of heavy rains, the call to caution came at 1 a.m., May 28. By 3 a.m., many homes and businesses had nearly four feet of water in their basements. With the water still rising at 4 a.m., many had to be rescued by boats. Many farm animals were lost in the sweeping water. (Submitted by Marilyn Johnson)

#42. Cor. W 7th & Sioux Sts. May 28, 1908.